1944

This book may be kept

THE POETICAL CAREER
OF ALEXANDER POPE

Mr. Pope.

The *Poetical* *Career*

of

ALEXANDER
POPE

By ROBERT KILBURN ROOT

1938: *PRINCETON*
PRINCETON UNIVERSITY PRESS

LONDON
HUMPHREY MILFORD, OXFORD UNIVERSITY PRESS

PRINTED AT THE PRINCETON UNIVERSITY PRESS
PRINCETON, NEW JERSEY, U. S. A.

PREFACE

OF ALL our English poets none has suffered more in his reputation from shiftings of literary taste than has Alexander Pope. To his delighted contemporaries he was the "Prince of English Poets," his throne on the topmost peak of the English Parnassus. In the nineteenth century critics could dispute as to whether he was really a poet at all. Since the beginning of the present century there have been many indications that the tide of taste has turned the other way. People are now disposed to like rather than to distrust the eighteenth century. Though no one, I imagine, would restore Pope to the supreme eminence which was his two hundred years ago, there are few lovers of our older literature who do not recognize him as a very considerable poet. But if the prejudice has disappeared, there remains much in the poetic art of Pope that needs for modern readers interpretation and fresh appraisal.

I have tried in the series of essays which make up this book to give such an interpretation and appraisal of Pope's art in its more important manifestations. Though the essays are for the most part arranged in such an order as to suggest the progress of his literary career, no attempt has been made to recount the events of his life, his warm friendships and bitter enmities, except as such matters may contribute immediately to an understanding of his poetry. I hope, however, that the frequent quotations from his correspondence and from such biographical sources as Spence's Anecdotes, while illustrating his *literary tastes and his methods of literary work, may also reveal something of his personal character, a character which is, I believe, in spite of some obvious defects, both lovable and noble.*

The chapter on the Dunciad *of 1729 is reprinted, though with numerous revisions, from an introduction which I wrote for a facsimile edition of the original quarto issued by the Princeton University Press in 1929. To the staff of the Huntington Library at San Marino, California, who in the summers of 1936 and 1937 made available to me its extraordinary treasures of printed books and manuscript materials, I owe a deep debt of gratitude. In particular I would acknowledge permission to reproduce as frontispiece to this book the engraved portrait, in perfect state, from the Hoe copy of the 1717 folio of Pope's* Works, *now in the Huntington Library.*

My obligations to other students of Pope are indicated in the Notes; but I wish particularly to record my debt to the work of Professor Griffith, Professor Sherburn, and M. Audra. Mr. Tillotson's illuminating essay, On the Poetry of Pope, *reached me after most of my book was already in type.*

CONTENTS

I

THE CANONS OF POETIC ART

To the average reader of today the world of poetry may well seem to be a region quite remote from the affairs of his own workaday world. He has wandered, not without bewilderment, through the forests and enchantments drear of the *Faery Queene*, or he has mounted up with Milton's Satan through the stormy void of dread Chaos and old Night. He has pursued Wordsworth to his lonely seclusion at Grasmere. He has with Byron sailed a pirate sloop among the Isles of Greece, or has explored those caverns measureless to man and that deep romantic chasm of Kubla Khan's magic garden. In much of the poetry of the present century, English and American, he has been baffled by the lawlessness and obscurity of what is only another phase of that many-headed thing which we call romanticism.

The poetry of Pope is something very different. Pope would have been quite miserable if doomed to live in the remoteness of a Dove Cottage; he had no desire to travel the road to Xanadu. For him order was a cardinal virtue, and obscurity a particularly deadly sin. He chose to live, not quite in the "eternal roar" of London, but so near at hand that his life was urban rather than rural. There is about him always an unmistakable urbanity; he is the thoroughly sophisticated man of the world, and from the world about him, from its conversation, its gossip and light badinage, came the substance of much of his verse.

I

If one is to read the work of Pope "with the same spirit that its author writ," one must make the effort to look at poetry through his eyes—at the poets who were for him the accepted masters and exemplars of the craft, and at that consensus of critical opinion which for him and for his generation set forth what poetry ought to be.

In the year 1700, when Pope was a little boy of twelve, his father acquired the small estate at Binfield on the western edge of Windsor Forest, which was to be the family home for the next sixteen years, and the scene of Pope's literary apprenticeship. He was an apprentice without any settled master; for at about this time, as he told Spence (p. 193), his regular schooling came to an end. To a boy of Roman Catholic faith the doors of public school and university were inexorably closed. Even had there been no legal proscription, the life of a public school would hardly have been possible for the frail little cripple. There was from time to time a priest domesticated in the household to act as desultory tutor for the lad; but for the most part he was his own schoolmaster. He had no need of any urging to mind his books. He read with insatiable appetite.

When I had done with my priests, I took to reading by myself, for which I had a very great eagerness and

> enthusiasm, especially for poetry: and in a few years I
> had dipped into a great number of English, French,
> Italian, Latin, and Greek poets. . . . These five or
> six years I still look upon as the happiest part of my
> life. (Spence, p. 193)
>
> In [this period], I went through all the best critics;
> almost all the English, French, and Latin poets of any
> name: the minor poets, Homer, and some of the
> greater Greek poets, in the original; and Tasso and
> Ariosto in translations. (Spence, p. 279)

The lonely little boy was not only voraciously reading poetry, he was also busily writing it.

> I wrote things—I'm ashamed to say how soon.—
> Part of an Epic Poem when about twelve. The scene
> of it lay at Rhodes, and some of the neighbouring
> islands; and the poem opened under water with a de-
> scription of the Court of Neptune. (Spence, p. 25)
>
> I endeavoured, (said he, smiling), in this poem to
> collect all the beauties of the great epic writers into
> one piece: there was Milton's style in one part, and
> Cowley's in another; here the style of Spenser
> imitated, and there of Statius; here Homer and Virgil,
> and there Ovid and Claudian. (Spence, p. 277)

During these years of eager and enthusiastic reading Pope "went through almost all the English poets
of any name." Who were they? How did the pageant
of English poetry display itself to a reader of the years
immediately after 1700? So much of English poetry
as we think of it had not yet been written; and the
rest fell into a very different perspective, and was
appraised by quite another set of critical ideas. We
look back at our older poets through the vista of the
nineteenth century—the Victorian era and the

Georgian—crowded with names of excellent poetic
note, and through the less splendid reaches of eighteenth-century poetry. For us both eighteenth century
and nineteenth are modern, at least in the sense that
the forms of the language and its literary style are not
noticeably different from our own. For the young
Pope all this did not exist.

For him, as for us, Shakespeare stands in the first
place. He is the supreme example of original genius,
who drew his art "immediately from the fountains of
Nature."

> The Poetry of *Shakespear* was Inspiration indeed:
> he is not so much an Imitator, as an Instrument, of
> Nature; and 'tis not so just to say that he speaks
> from her, as that she speaks thro' him.

He has an unequalled power over our passions, so
that the reader's "heart swells, and the tears burst
out, just at the proper places." But "with all these
great excellencies, he has almost as great defects."
Forced to cater to the untrained taste of his mean and
vulgar audience, he gives us in tragedy "the most
strange, unexpected, and consequently most unnatural, Events and Incidents: the most exaggerated
Thoughts; the most verbose and bombast Expression;
the most pompous Rhymes, and thundering Versification." In comedy he descends to "mean buffoonery,
vile ribaldry, and unmannerly jests of fools and
clowns."

> Yet even in these, our Author's Wit buoys up, and
> is born above his subject: his Genius in those low

parts is like some Prince of a Romance in the disguise
of a Shepherd or Peasant: a certain Greatness and
Spirit now and then break out, which manifest his
higher extraction and qualities.[1]

Pope could do full reverence to the greatness and
spirit of Shakespeare's genius; but it would not have
occurred to him that Shakespeare could in any sense
serve as poetic model for an age of enlightened and
exacting taste.

Apart from the drama, there were just four English
poets who could in any sense be regarded as great
masters. "Chaucer, Spenser, Milton, and Dryden,"
Pope said to Spence, "are the great land-marks" of
our poetry. (p. 171.) Dryden was dead but yesterday.
Pope had, indeed, seen his living figure, had with wide-
open boyish eyes looked reverently at him enthroned
on his favourite tavern chair.[2] *Paradise Lost*, first
published in 1667, was but some thirty-five years old.
In Pope's boyhood, Spenser and Shakespeare were, in
years, not so far off as are Byron and Shelley from us.
Though Chaucer was, as measured by the calendar,
two centuries nearer than he is to us, on the score of
sympathy and understanding he was much farther
removed.

Chaucer to his contemporaries had been the
English Virgil, the pattern of perfected literary art;
to the Elizabethans he was the English Homer, the
pattern of "nature" rather than of "art," the great
poet of an unsophisticated age; by the year 1700 he
had become the English Ennius, the rude pioneer of

English verse. In that very year Samuel Wesley in an *Epistle to a Friend concerning Poetry* wrote:[3]

> Of CHAUCER's Verse we scarce the *Measures* know,
> So *rough* the *Lines*, and so *unequal* flow;
> Whether by Injury of *Time* defac'd,
> Or *careless* at the *first*, and writ in *haste;*
> Or *coursly*, like old *Ennius*, he design'd
> What After-days have *polish'd* and *refin'd*.

Even Dryden, in the Preface to the *Fables* published in the same year, mingles with his glowing tribute to Chaucer as "a perpetual Fountain of good Sense," and as "a Man of a most wonderful comprehensive Nature," no small measure of condescension for the rudeness of his language and verse: *"Chaucer*, I confess, is a rough Diamond; and must first be polish'd e'er he shines." And Pope himself in the *Essay on Criticism*, bewailing the instability of our English speech, takes Chaucer as the type of the completely obsolete:

> And such as Chaucer is, shall Dryden be.   (483)

On which Pope's carping critic, John Dennis, remarks that Dryden had "acquired some Justness of Numbers and some Truth of Harmony and of Versification, to which Chaucer thro' the Rudeness of the Language, or want of Ear, or want of Experience, or rather perhaps a mixture of all, could not possibly attain."

It is a pity that Dryden and Pope could not have read Chaucer in a less corrupted text, with the understanding of his language and verse that we have today, and with a better realization of the world in which he lived. For Chaucer, as we may read him, measures up extraordinarily well to those critical canons to which Dryden and Pope gave allegiance.

Pope's understanding of Chaucer was very much less adequate than was Dryden's. It seems to have been "Chaucer's worst ribaldry" (*To Augustus*, 37) which left the deepest impress on his memory. His youthful "imitation" of Chaucer is a very ribald jest; he chose for "translation" the *Merchant's Tale* and the *Wife of Bath's Prologue*. It would be difficult to show that Pope's poetry, apart from the *Temple of Fame*, is in any essential quality derived from Chaucer.

The same is, I think, true for Spenser, despite the fact that Pope read him with "infinite delight." In the year before his death, Pope said to Spence:

> After reading a canto of Spenser two or three days ago to an old lady, between seventy and eighty years of age, she said that I had been showing her a gallery of pictures.—I don't know how it is, but she said very right: there is something in Spenser that pleases one as strongly in one's old age, as it did in one's youth. I read the Faerie Queene, when I was about twelve, with infinite delight; and I think it gave me as much, when I read it over about a year or two ago. (p. 296)

But if in Spenser Pope found perpetual delight, he found also much to offend his critical taste. If Spenser had great virtues, he also had great faults (*To Augustus*, 95-7), chief among which was his affectation of the obsolete. Despite the nearness of time, Spenser's diction would have seemed to Pope more affected than it does to us; for many of his obsolete words and phrases, both those which he affected and those which belong to his own generation, acquired in the nineteenth century new poetic currency, through imitation of Spenser himself and because of the literary vogue of romantic strangeness. Spenser could delight Pope, both in his boyhood and in his latest years, by his "gallery of pictures"; but his "forests and enchantments drear," his dragons and his giants were hardly a "following of nature." The marvels of Spenser's fairyland must after his boyhood days have seemed to Pope mere "romantic nonsense," redeemed into any sort of poetic seriousness only by their allegorical significance. Pope's early "imitation" of Spenser is a playful parody; and the Cave of Spleen in the fourth canto of the *Rape of the Lock* is in much the same temper.

To Milton, on the other hand, Pope's artistic indebtedness is of considerable importance, and that in spite of their total dissimilarity of character. He knew *Paradise Lost* with the intimacy of complete appropriation. Professor Havens's list of Miltonic echoes in Pope's poetry is a long and impressive one.[4] He recognized fully Milton's greatness. He wrote to his friend Caryll on June 25, 1711:

> I keep the pictures of Dryden, Milton, Shakespeare, &c., in my chamber, round about me, that the constant remembrance of them may keep me always humble.

But Milton's defects, his not infrequent lapses from

poetic taste, are of a sort which made them to Pope particularly repugnant:

> Milton's strong pinion now not Heav'n can bound,
> Now Serpent-like, in prose he sweeps the ground,
> In Quibbles, Angel and Archangel join,
> And God the Father turns a School-divine.
>
> (To Augustus, 99-102)

Though the diction of *Paradise Lost* exerted an unmistakable influence on Pope's own diction, particularly in his translations of Homer, yet it seemed to him overstrained in its studied elevation. "Milton's style, in his *Paradise Lost*, is not natural; 'tis an exotic style," he said to Spence in 1734. (p. 174.) And three years later he said again to Spence:

> The high style, that is affected so much in blank verse, would not have been borne, even in Milton, had not his subject turned so much on such strange out-of-the-world things as it does. (p. 200)

Not only Milton's style, but the "strange out-of-the-world" substance of his poetry, raised in Pope's mind the query as to whether Milton has duly "followed nature."

Of the four poets who, with Shakespeare, were for Pope the great land-marks of our poetry, Dryden was, if not in his judgment the greatest, certainly the most fully in accord with Pope's temper and with his critical principles. He is the first great English poet whom Pope could regard as "polite," as possessing that cultivated urbanity which is one of the fine flowers of a settled social order.

> We conquer'd France, but felt our Captive's charms;
> Her Arts victorious triumph'd o'er our Arms;

Britain to soft refinements less a foe,
Wit grew polite, and Numbers learn'd to flow.
Waller was smooth; but Dryden taught to join
The varying verse, the full-resounding line,
The long majestic March, and Energy divine.
Tho' still some traces of our rustic vein
And splay-foot verse, remain'd, and will remain.
Late, very late, correctness grew our care,
When the tir'd Nation breath'd from civil war.
Exact Racine, and Corneille's noble fire,
Show'd us that France had something to admire.
Not but the Tragic spirit was our own,
And full in Shakespear, fair in Otway shone:
But Otway fail'd to polish or refine,
And fluent Shakespear scarce effac'd a line.
Ev'n copious Dryden wanted, or forgot,
The last and greatest Art, the Art to blot.

(*To Augustus*, 264-81)

The poets before Dryden had been rich in poetic
"genius"—Shakespeare to a degree unrivalled, unless
by Homer—but they had been deficient in poetic art,
in that perfect grace of utterance which is the characteristic note of Virgil, and, though to a less degree, of
the "exact Racine." Virgil and Racine are preemi-
nently "polite," informed by a serene urbanity of
spirit and manner. In Spenser, in the "divine" Shakespeare, in Milton, Pope found an extravagance and
turbulence of spirit and an uncouthness of diction
which savoured of the provincial rather than of the
urbane. They are noble and highly gifted barbarians
beyond the limits of the *pax Romana*. Even Dryden
shows "still some traces of our rustic vein."

Mr. Walsh, one of the literary mentors of Pope's
adolescence, had said to him that "though we had

several great poets, we never had any one great poet that was *correct*." (Spence, p. 280.) What this forbidding word meant to Pope, and presumably to Walsh, we shall have occasion to inquire presently. Dryden had been a pioneer in refinement and correctness; it was Pope's early ambition to make English poetry wholly urbane.

It is important, then, to remember that though Pope honoured the great poets of an earlier generation, honoured them in spite of their defects, their vein of rusticity, he thought of his own generation as leading a new poetic movement, initiated at the Restoration, but hitherto only partially realized. Like Wordsworth and Coleridge a century later, he was eager to reform English poetry, to purge it of its errors and set it in the path of artistic truth.

II

During those early years of voracious reading in his father's house at Binfield, Pope "went through" not only the chief European poets but "all the best critics" also. Who the "best critics" were is made clear in the concluding section of the *Essay on Criticism*. They were inevitably the critics who make up that tradition which we label as "classical":— Aristotle, Horace, Quintilian, Longinus, Vida, the "critic-learning" that flourished in seventeenth-century France—Rapin, Le Bossu, Boileau[5]—and those English critics of the Restoration—

> Who durst assert the juster ancient cause,
> And here restor'd Wit's fundamental laws.
> (*Essay on Criticism*, 721-2)

When we apply the convenient label "classical" or "neo-classical" to the critical theories of seventeenth-century France, we run the risk inherent in all such convenient labelling of assuming a quite fallacious unity in the materials to which the label is affixed. Actually no such uniformity exists. In opposition to later critical theories such as those of Coleridge or those of Croce, there may be a measure of agreement sufficient to justify the inclusive label; but the French critics of the seventeenth century were far indeed from harmonious agreement. There was room in plenty for acrimonious dispute within their ranks. The famous controversy of Ancients *versus* Moderns, a controversy much more significant in the principles involved than some later historians have been aware,[6] was a quarrel among critics all of whom we should label as "neo-classical."

Within this body of critical opinion one can distinguish at least three schools of thought, or, since no single critic can be pointed out as owing exclusive allegiance to any one of them, it is better to say three dominating principles of criticism, which may be designated as the Principle of Authority, the Principle of Reason and Good Sense, and the Principle of Taste. So essentially at variance are these three principles that it took all the ingenuity of a Boileau to bring them into some semblance of harmony.

The Principle of Authority actuates that aspect of seventeenth-century criticism which has best claim to the label "classicism." It rests upon the premise that the great poets of Greece and Rome had attained a pitch of artistic perfection which no modern poet can hope to equal, still less surpass. These ancient altars are "above the reach of sacrilegious hands."

> Hail, Bards triumphant! born in happier days;
> Immortal heirs of universal praise!
> Whose honours with increase of ages grow.
>   .   .   .   .
> Oh may some spark of your celestial fire
> The last, the meanest of your sons inspire,
> (That on weak wings, from far, pursues your flights;
> Glows while he reads, but trembles as he writes).
>
> (*Essay on Criticism*, 189-98)

The poets of antiquity are, as it were, the church "triumphant," in full possession of the beatific vision of true poetic art. The devout modern will in humility of heart invoke their intercession, and hope that he may have the grace to follow their good examples. He will imitate, if not the substance of their writings, at least the spirit which informs them; he will check his own poetic procedure by reference to theirs, he will give due regard to "those Rules of old discovered, not devised," in which Aristotle and the continuators of the Aristotelian tradition formulated their poetic procedure.

> Hear how learn'd *Greece* her useful rules indites,
> When to repress, and when indulge our flights!
>   .   .   .   .
> Just precepts thus from great examples giv'n,
> She drew from them what they derived from heav'n.
>
> (*Essay on Criticism*, 92-9)

Fundamentally opposed to this principle is the Principle of Reason and Good Sense. Rationalism is of necessity arrayed against authority. It is the first

tenet of Cartesian rationalism "never to accept anything as true which I do not recognize evidently to be
so." In its most extreme and uncompromising form,
rationalism would wish to deal with all things as one
deals with a problem in mathematics, where reason is
all in all. However we may feel about the hypotenuse,
we cannot make it more nor less than the squares of
the other two sides may determine; we do not indulge
in lyric rapture over the perfection of an isosceles
triangle. We must hold to the truth, and the sanction
of truth is the human reason; we shall therefore distrust sentiment, and emotion, and pleasing illusion,
which are the secular enemies of reason.

When the supremacy of reason is brought into the
field of literary criticism, certain results will necessarily follow. A poem is something other than a
demonstration in Euclid, but it must be able to stand
a rational scrutiny no less inexorable; it must be not
only beautiful but just. And its truth and justice, no
less than its beauty, must be immediately recognizable to all men, everywhere, and in all ages.

If it is to be immediately apprehended by any competent reader, a poem must be free from all obscurity
of conception or of expression, from all vagueness or
blurring of outline. If it is to appeal to all men everywhere, it must have an idealized universality, must
deal with the general rather than the minutely particular, must transcend all idiosyncrasies and personal prejudices. If human reason is a constant, the
same, if rightly used, in the age of Pericles, of Augustus, of Louis XIV, the same in Greece, in England, in

China and Peru, a poem should, to satisfy the demands of reason, be as far as possible placeless and
timeless. Local colour and historical perspective thus
become blemishes rather than virtues.

All this is comprehended in the great all-inclusive
"rule" that a poet must "follow nature":

> First follow Nature, and your judgment frame
> By her just standard, which is still the same:
> Unerring NATURE, still divinely bright,
> One clear, unchang'd, and universal light,
> Life, force, and beauty, must to all impart,
> At once the source, and end, and test of Art.
>
> (*Essay on Criticism*, 68-73)

Pope is here addressing the critic, but he would have
regarded the lines as equally suitable for the poet. A
great deal is packed into them. Nature is justly
ordered, constant, unerring, universal; her light is the
clear light of day, obscured by no mist or shadows, not
broken by any prism into the spectral particularities
of blue, yellow, and red. It is plain that the Nature
that the poet must follow is something very different
from the Nature to which Rousseau would have had
us return. It is not rude and simple, but rather the
highly organized, ideally ordered, system of things,
from which all accidental aberrations have been
eliminated. Its breath is not that of the wild west
wind, blowing where it listeth, but of the steadily
directed trades. For Rousseau and the Romantics the
opposite of the natural is the artificial, the sophisticated; for the neo-classical critic the opposite of the
natural is the abnormal. For him the life of the normal
civilized man in court and city is more in accord with

Nature than is the less organized life of the rustic. What we shall ask of a poem, then, is this: Does it present in clear and appropriate language a just picture of a normal, universal aspect of life? Does it embody in images of precise accuracy a significant general truth? Are its sentiments such as to find an immediate echo in every normal human breast?

By the test of reason and common sense, conceived in any such downright fashion as this, much of the poetry of Greece and Rome will fare rather badly. Homer in particular abounds in the irrationally marvelous. His speaking horses were a stumbling block to many a seventeenth-century critic. According to La Motte the heroes of the *Iliad* are coarse and brutal, vain-glorious and cruel; the gods are ignorant, unjust, at the mercy of their passions—"méprisable de quelque côte qu'on les considère." Is it thus that right reason conceives of gods and heroes?[7]

The two conflicting principles of Authority and Reason serve admirably as correctives to one another. Reason and Good Sense prevent too servile an imitation of the Ancients, too absolute a reliance on the Rules as final and authoritative pronouncements. The indisputable greatness of the Greek and Latin poets stands as perpetual antidote to a cold and barren rationalism. Most of the critics—and Pope is among their number—seek to effect a compromise between these opposing principles. With one critic the compromise will lean towards reason, with another towards authority. The Rules, as Pope reminds us, were "discovered not devised," discovered by the human reason. They are "nature methodized," a set of codified directions to guide the reason in its following of Nature. Pope imagines the young Virgil setting pen to the *Æneid* in proud independence of literary models and the critic's law, scorning to draw except from the fountains of Nature herself:

> But when t'examine ev'ry part he came,
> Nature and *Homer* were, he found, the same.
>
> (*Essay on Criticism*, 134-5)

So completely have the great poets of antiquity succeeded in their following of Nature, that Nature speaks through them. If one could conform one's spirit to theirs, one would attain perfect reasonableness and good sense, perfect naturalness:

> Learn hence for ancient rules a just esteem;
> To copy nature is to copy them.
>
> (*Essay on Criticism*, 139-40)

Thomas Rymer, chiefly remembered for his completely wrong-headed critique of *Othello*, in which the appeal to good sense results in arrant nonsense, wishing to carry the waters of criticism on both shoulders, entitles his book (published 1678): "The Tragedies of the Last Age [i.e. of the age of Elizabeth and James I] Consider'd and Examin'd by the practice of the Ancients and by the Common Sense of All Ages."

The famous controversy of Ancients and Moderns is basically the conflict between the principle of Authority and the principle of Reason. Though it begot on both sides much partisan absurdity, it was in itself of real significance. It is in effect the same conflict that we have today between those who would build on the tradition which has flowed down to us from the past and those who, delighting in their modernity, are content to depend on nothing but their own ingenuity. Swift's spider spins cobweb from the "native stock within himself"; his bee "by a universal range, with long search, much study, true judgment, and distinction of things, brings home honey and wax . . . thus furnishing mankind with the two noblest of things, which are sweetness and light."

Besides the principles of Reason and Authority, there is a third principle which enters into the composite of neo-classical criticism, as formulated by Boileau and passed on by him to Pope, the principle of Taste. Taste is essentially different from Reason and Authority. They, though sharply at variance with one another, still are in accord in seeking for external criteria by which a work of art may be judged. Taste is a matter of immediate intuition, which does not admit of logical dispute. The principle of Taste protests against servile obedience to the Rules, whether dictated by Authority or formulated by Reason. It looks for those "nameless graces which no methods teach"; it "snatches a grace beyond the reach of art," and so "gains the heart" (*Essay on Criticism*, 144-55); it gives to a poem an indefinable charm, the *Je ne sçais quoi*. Always a liberalizing tendency, it would, if given sole sway, amount to uncontrolled impressionism. In its origins it was hardly distinguishable from impressionism; but it was speedily to become a rather tame rebel. It appeals from strict observance of the Rules by pleading the precedent of the ancient authors who "gloriously offend" against them. Or it seeks support in Longinus and his *furor poeticus* as against the more methodized criticism of Aristotle and Horace. It thus makes peace with Authority. In the controversy of Ancients *versus* Moderns the adherents of Taste are likely to be found on the side of the Ancients. But it is also reconciled with Reason. For the taste of the individual, which is mere impressionism, is substituted the universalized taste of all competent judges. It seeks, as in Pope's fourth *Moral Essay*, to support its intuitions by the criteria of usefulness and good sense. As Pope says in the prefatory argument to the epistle: "The first principle and foundation, in this [Taste] as in everything else, is *Good Sense*. The chief proof of it is to *follow Nature*." (The italics are Pope's.) It becomes thus almost a synonym of Good Sense; but it never quite loses its identity, keeps always some flavour of freedom. It looks for the savour—and the fire—of true poetic art; it is concerned to find the beauties of a poem rather than to point out its faults. Its heaviest censure is to call a poem dull.

III

It has been possible to illustrate the various aspects of the neo-classical tradition by quotations from Pope's *Essay on Criticism*; for what Pope has done in the *Essay* is to give new and striking expression to the oft-repeated commonplaces of "all the best critics," adopting for himself an eclectic reconciliation of their divergent positions closely similar to that of his more particular master, Boileau. As Addison said in a kindly notice of the poem in *Spectator* 253, published December 20, 1711, some seven months after the appearance of the poem:

> The Observations follow one another like those in *Horace's Art of Poetry*, without that methodical Regularity which would have been requisite in a Prose Author. They are some of them uncommon, but such as the Reader must assent to, when he sees them explained with that Elegance and Perspicuity in which they are delivered. As for those which are the most known, and the most received, they are placed in so beautiful a Light, and illustrated with such apt Allusions, that they have in them all the Graces of novelty, and make the Reader, who was before acquainted with them, still more convinced of their Truth and Solidity.

If the *Essay on Criticism* contains little that is Pope's own except the felicity of its expression, it must not be forgotten that it is the work of a very young man. It was published in May, 1711; on the twenty-first of that month Pope completed his twenty-third year. This first edition, reissued with slight differences on the title page on January 1, 1712, did not bear the author's name. The second edition (1713) contains on the title the phrase "Written by Mr. Pope." Later editions give the further statement: "Written in the year 1709." In the years 1734-1736 Pope said to Spence (p. 170): "My Essay on Criticism was written in 1709; and published in 1711; which is as little time as ever I let anything of mine lay by me." It was, if written in 1709, a sufficiently precocious achievement

for a young gentleman of twenty-one. But Pope was
not satisfied; a few years later he told Spence (p. 194)
that he had shown the poem to his friend and mentor,
Walsh, "in 1706. Walsh died the year after."[8] Though
Pope is notoriously unreliable in his chronological
utterances, there is no inherent unlikelihood that an
early draft of the poem, or of some passages of it, may
have been shown as early as 1706 to the friend to
whose memory he pays such glowing tribute near the
end of the poem as we now know it. In 1706, Pope was
a boy of eighteen.

In Part III of the *Essay*, where Pope is discussing
"Rules for the Conduct of *Manners* in a Critic," are
found the lines:

> But *Appius* reddens at each word you speak,
> And stares, tremendous, with a threat'ning eye,
> Like some fierce Tyrant in old Tapestry.

It was obvious to everyone that the lines were directed
at the middle-aged critic, John Dennis, author of a
piece called *Appius and Virginia*, in whose vocabulary
the word "tremendous" was a much overworked
vocable. But I imagine that it was the youthfulness
of the author quite as much as the ridicule of these
lines which enraged Mr. Dennis. Who is this young
upstart who with a glib tongue presumes to lay down
the law for literary critics?

Whatever the predominant motive, there can be no
doubt about the rage. The *Essay on Criticism* had
been out only a little more than a month when, on
June 20, 1711, Dennis published his *Reflections
Critical and Satyrical upon a late Rhapsody Call'd An*

Essay upon Criticism. It is a very angry and ill-natured pamphlet. It points out many inconsistencies and confusions in detail. Some of the objections are sound—and of many of these Pope took advantage in his later revisions; others are mere carping querulousness, which overlooks the fact that the *Essay* is a graceful poem rather than a solemn treatise in prose. The significance of Dennis's pamphlet lies in this, that a very angry hostile critic should have limited his attack to matters of detail, and should have found nothing to censure in essential substance except "the Servile Deference which he pays to the Ancients."[9] The critical principles which Pope has formulated were, apparently, matters of such universal acceptation that Dennis, like Addison, could not but be "convinced of their truth and solidity."

To any well informed reader perusing the poem without Dennis's animus it must have been evident that young Mr. Pope had produced a poetical "essay" as brilliant and as "solid" as Boileau's *Art Poétique*, something incomparably finer than Mulgrave's *Essay on Poetry* (1682), Roscommon's *Essay on Translated Verse* (1684), or Lord Lansdowne's *Essay upon Unnatural Flights in Poetry* (1701), the only English poems with which it could be compared. An attentive reader would have recognized in the recently published poem some echoes from these "noble lords," and would have noted that the debt to the critics of seventeenth-century France included happy phrases as well as general principles. Rapin had said of

Aristotle (and Dryden in his Preface to *Troilus and Cressida* had echoed the phrase):

> En effet sa Poétique n'est à proprement parler, que la nature mise en méthode, et le bon sens réduit en principes. (*Réflexions sur la Poétique*: Préface)

And Pope's definition of "true wit" as "what oft was thought but ne'er so well expressed" owes everything but its perfect conciseness to Boileau's Preface to the 1701 edition of his works:

> Qu'est ce qu'une pensée neuve, brillante, extra-ordinaire? Ce n'est point, comme se persuadent les ignorants, une pensée que personne n'a jamais eue, ni dû avoir. C'est au contraire une pensée qui a dû venir à tout le monde, et que quelqu'un s'avise le premier d'exprimer. Un bon mot n'est bon mot qu'en ce qu'il dit une chose que chacun pensoit, et qu'il la dit d'une manière vive, fine, et nouvelle.

The only originality of substance to which the *Essay* can lay claim lies in the fact that it is not an "art of poetry" but an "art of criticism"—or rather an "essay" towards such a treatise. It does not, like Boileau and Mulgrave, consider in order the various "kinds" of poetry—tragedy and epic, elegy and ode. Instead of a "progress" of poesy there is in Part III a progress of criticism from Greece to Rome, to France, to England. And much of the good advice is applicable only to the critic rather than to the poet. One will be in danger of misinterpreting the poem if one forgets that Pope is throughout speaking in the first instance to the critic. That will explain the continual insistence on the need of good sense, which every one will agree is a virtue indispensable to the critic—though in our estimation today, at any rate, secondary among the qualities which make the poet. It is the critic rather than the poet for whom a little learning is so dangerous a thing.

But though the *Essay* is concerned primarily with criticism, an art of poetry is inevitably there by implication; for the good critic, if not himself a poet, must have qualities closely akin. The theory of good poetry is more essential to his function than it is to that of the poet. Shakespeare, as Pope and his generation regarded him, could by sheer force of genius be a very great (though imperfect) poet, despite his total ignorance of the Rules. But knowledge of the Rules alone will not make one a critic. The critic, like the poet, must be born, not made:

> In Poets as true Genius is but rare,
> True Taste as seldom is the Critic's share;
> Both must alike from heav'n derive their light,
> These born to judge, as well as those to write.
>
> (*Essay on Criticism*, 11-14)

If there is in the *Essay* much emphasis on the need of more than a little learning, it must be remembered that it is this inborn quality of Taste which is the *sine qua non*. True Taste is as indispensable to the critic as true Genius to the poet.

It was Pope's early ambition to be not only a great poet but a "correct" poet. The word is, for our modern ears, an unfortunate one, which suggests the literary priggishness of frigid impeccability. Pope has himself vigorously condemned—

> . . . such lays as neither ebb, nor flow,
> Correctly cold, and regularly low,
> That shunning faults, one quiet tenour keep;
> We cannot blame indeed—but we may sleep.
>
> (*Essay on Criticism*, 239-42)

The "correctness" which Pope was ambitious to attain involved more than mere freedom from faults; it was a positive rather than a negative quality. Word and phrase must be not only free from offense but exquisitely right; the numbers must have precisely the melody and tone which shall "seem an Echo to the Sense." There must be complete truth to "nature"— no strained exaggeration, no vague unreality, perfect sanity, clarity not only in expression but in conception. The poetic fire must burn steadily and brightly, without smoke or explosive spluttering. It is obvious that by such tests as these Spenser, Shakespeare, and Milton too frequently fall short of "correctness." Could Pope have read him with the understanding possible to us today, he would have found in Chaucer an English poet who was not only a "great" poet, but to an extraordinary degree also a "correct" poet.

"Correctness," the perfect "following of nature," demands in the poet a nice balance of the two faculties into which the critical analysis of Pope and of his generation distinguished the act of literary creation, a nice balance between Wit and Judgment. "Wit" is a very elusive term, which is used in the *Essay on Criticism* with more than a single meaning. The word

176 12

occurs forty-three times in the course of the poem. Most often it is used (twenty-two times) without precise definition in the sense of "literary art," or (twelve times) in the sense of "man-of-letters." Four times (lines 53, 61, 209, 429, and by implication in line 81) it has its original meaning of "intellectual power." Once (line 449) in the phrase "ready wit" it has its present-day meaning of "cleverness." When set in opposition to "judgment" (lines 28, 80, 82, 302, 303, 531) it takes on a more technical significance. It is then approximately equivalent to that aspect of literary creation which we call "fancy" or "imagination,"[10] which Pope in the Preface to the *Iliad* calls "invention"—a term which he there uses interchangeably with "fancy."[11] It is his supremacy in this faculty that gives to Homer first place in the hierarchy of the poets:

> The Praise of Judgment *Virgil* has justly contested with him, and others may have their Pretensions as to particular Excellencies; but his Invention remains yet unrival'd. Nor is it a Wonder if he has ever been acknowledg'd the greatest of Poets, who most excell'd in That which is the very Foundation of Poetry. It is the Invention that in different degrees distinguishes all great Genius's: The utmost Stretch of human Study, Learning, and Industry, which masters everything besides, can never attain to this. It furnishes Art with all her Materials, and without it Judgment itself can at best but *steal wisely*: for Art is only like a prudent Steward that lives on managing the Riches of Nature. Whatever Praises may be given to Works of Judgment, there is not even a single Beauty in them but is owing to the Invention. (Fol. B, recto and verso)

It is Invention which gives to a poem poetic fire:

> Exact Disposition, just Thought, correct Elocution, polish'd Numbers, may have been found in a thousand; but this Poetical *Fire*, this *Vivida vis animi*, in a very few. (Fol. B 2, verso)

It is Wit or Invention that can alone kindle the flame; it is the function of Judgment to tend the fire, to see that it shall burn clear and bright, that it shall not become an uncontrolled conflagration. Wit is the *vivida vis animi*, the life-blood of poetry, but—

> Works may have more wit than does 'em good
> As bodies perish thro' excess of blood.
>
> *(Essay on Criticism*, 303-4)

Even in Homer, Invention sometimes outruns controlling Judgment, so that Pope must admit that "some things are too luxuriant." When extolling the greatness of Homer's poetry, Pope gives clear primacy to Invention as opposed to Judgment—and this was presumably his settled opinion; but in the *Essay on Criticism* the emphasis is rather on the dangers of too profuse a Wit, a Wit not disciplined by Judgment.

> For wit and judgment often are at strife,
> Tho' meant each other's aid, like man and wife.
> 'Tis more to guide, than spur the Muse's steed;
> Restrain his fury, than provoke his speed;
> The winged courser, like a gen'rous horse,
> Shows most true mettle when you check his course.
>
> *(Essay on Criticism*, 82-6)

Pegasus must be a "generous horse," no mere plodding nag; but his *vivida vis animi* is best shown when the expert horseman rides him with a tight rein, hold-

ing him to the intended road. The horse that bore
Byron's Mazeppa—

> Was a noble steed,
> A Tartar of the Ukraine breed,
> Who looked as though the speed of thought
> Were in his limbs; but he was wild,
> Wild as the wild deer, and untaught,
> With spur and bridle undefiled.

Mazeppa, helplessly bound on his back, is carried
headlong over pathless wastes, "Torrents less rapid
and less rash," wherever the maddened courser sees a
way. The ride of Mazeppa is a fitting symbol of the
extreme form of that poetry which we call romantic.
Could Pope have read Shelley—the *Prometheus* for
example—he would have marveled at the poet's overflowing abundance of Wit and would have lamented
the lack of controlling Judgment. The conceits of
the "metaphysical" poets of the seventeenth century
seemed to him—

> One glaring Chaos and wild heap of wit.

The ideal is a perfect balance of Wit and Judgment.
If Wit is deficient, the poem will be dull and lifeless; if
Judgment fails, the result will be extravagance and
absurdity, a departure from the "just standards" of
"unerring Nature."

Though Pope both in the *Essay on Criticism* and in
the Preface to the *Iliad* exalts Homer above Virgil, his
own taste and temper, and the prevailing taste of his
generation, is Latin rather than Greek. However high
he may rank the faculty of Invention, or Wit, the

allegiance of his spirit is given rather to the restraining faculty of Judgment, to the order and discipline
over which it presides. For him the truly golden age
is the age of Augustan Rome, the age of ordered peace.

The theories of literary art set forth in the *Essay on
Criticism* are those of a liberal and intelligent adherent of that school of poetry which we label neo-
classical. Though Pope pays glowing and eloquent
tribute to the "Bards triumphant" of ancient Greece
and Rome, he never suggests that poetic inspiration
ceased with them. In the *Epistle to Augustus* he makes
merry with those who would estimate poets on the
score of their antiquity to the utter dispraise of everything modern:

> Had ancient times conspir'd to disallow
> What then was new, what had been ancient now?

> (135-6)

Still less does he counsel imitation of the ancients,
except as one may seek to conform one's spirit to their
serenity and truth. Though there is no doubt in Pope's
mind that good sense is as indispensable in poetry as
in every other human activity, that the faculty of
rational thinking is as becoming to a poet as to any
other variety of *homo sapiens*, and that Wit un-
balanced by Judgment is likely to land one in confusion or uncertainty, he does not forget that the poet
must win his reader's heart as well as his head. There
is a "grace beyond the reach of art,"

> Which, without passing through the judgment, gains
> The heart, and all its end at once attains.

> (*Essay on Criticism*, 154-5)

To the Rules he pays homage as useful formulations of past poetic experience; but he never imagines that they alone can make one a good critic, still less a good poet. To exalt them beyond their proper value would have been to disown his national poetic birthright. It was no blind following of the Rules that had given us a Shakespeare, a Spenser, or even so essentially "classical" a poet as Milton. Pope could forget their "faults" in his whole-hearted admiration of their "beauties." For him the ultimate criterion of poetry is not a codified set of rules, but a sound and disciplined taste.

Poetry written in accordance with even so liberally held a neo-classicism as that of Pope will inevitably be marked by certain qualities which distinguish it from the poetry of those less ordered ages of Elizabeth and James on the one hand and of the romantic nineteenth century on the other.

Though in Pope's poetic theory clear primacy is given to the faculty which he calls Wit or Invention, the following of Nature demands that Wit be always accompanied by reflective Judgment. There will be quiet restraint rather than rapture and rhapsody. Pope's Muse will lead no mad Bacchanals; she is too civilized, too urbane, to play the Mænad. Poetic emotion will go hand in hand with poetic thought. Mere emotionalism, mere sensation without intellectual discipline and direction, will seem too cheap and easy an appeal to the mob spirit. To the invitation of unthinking sensation there is too ready a response. Pope and the Augustans sought to win not only the heart but the head. To read his close-knit couplets there must be alertness of mind as well as of imaginative sensation. A reader must have his "wits" about him.

If Horace Walpole's dictum be true, that life is a tragedy to those who feel, a comedy to those who think, we shall not be surprised that the prevailing temper of the Augustans is thoughtfully comic rather than deeply tragic. They were well aware that many things in their world were out of joint; but they tried to set things straight by a thoughtful laughter, sometimes kindly laughter, sometimes scornful, rather than by bitter outcry and loud lament.

The poetry which seeks first to "follow nature" will be chiefly concerned to find poetic truth in the familiar every-day world of actual men and women, as they transact their lives in the bustle of London or in the quiet English countryside. Except in the highly conventionalized unreality of the Pastoral, it will be an art of interpretation rather than of escape. It will open no magic casements giving on a world of imagination beyond ordinary experience, a world of mysterious shadows. It will prefer light rather than darkness, clear sunlight rather than the glimpses of the moon.

But it will not regard this actual world with particularized realism, but rather *sub quâdam specie æternitatis*, looking not for the freaks of nature but for her abiding types and forms.

THE HEROIC COUPLET

POPE is to an extraordinary degree the poet of a single verse-form. Very nearly the whole of his poetry is poured into the mould of the heroic couplet. The *Ode on St. Cecilia's Day* and the *Universal Prayer* are the only poems in any way memorable which forsake this single pattern.[1] The heroic quatrain of Dryden's *Annus Mirabilis* seems to have had no attraction for him. It was regarded as standing in the same relation to the heroic couplet that the Latin elegiac bears to the heroic hexameter. Long before Gray used it for his *Elegy*, it had taken on for eighteenth-century taste the tone of pensive melancholy. Pope might well have used it instead of the couplet for his *Elegy to the Memory of an Unfortunate Lady*. His early playful imitation of Spenser is his only attempt at the Spenserian stanza, and that despite the fact that Spenser was one of his favourite poets.

As his correspondence with Atterbury makes clear,[2] he had no hostility to blank verse; he could do full justice to Thomson's *Seasons*, and more than full justice to Akenside.[3] With both these poets he was on terms of friendly intercourse; to both he was generous in his help. His own projected epic about the British Brutus was to have been in blank verse, and a rough draft of its opening invocation has survived to us in manuscript.[4] The unique text contains several revisions; Pope's latest intention would seem to put the lines in the following form:

> The Patient Chief, who lab'ring long arriv'd
> On Britain's shores and brought with fav'ring Gods
> Arts, Arms, & Honour to her Ancient sons:
> Daughter of Memory! from elder Time
> Recall; and me with Britain's Glory fire,
> Me far from meaner Care, or meaner Song,
> Snatch to the Holy Hill of spotless Bay,
> My Country's Poet, to record her Fame.
>   Say first what Cause? that Pow'r h. . . .

These lines show that Pope could write blank verse at least as well as his friend, James Thomson; but not a single example of the form is found in his published verse. He did not even, like so many of his contemporaries, write a burlesque imitation of Milton's manner.

St. Cecilia is his only important essay at the "greater" ode,[5] that metrical safety-valve of neo-classical verse, and that poem is as dull in its modulations as in its conception. Only rarely did Pope use the octosyllabic couplet which was the favourite measure of his friend Swift.

This all but exclusive use of a single form, in sharp contrast with the practice of the major poets of the nineteenth century, has been one of the causes for the verdict of monotony so often rendered by hostile critics of his verse. For a reader who turns from Shelley or Tennyson to Pope, and merely leaves over a volume of his poetry, there is in the very look of the printed pages a somewhat forbidding uniformity.

Nor is that the whole of the matter. This single form is of a narrowly restricted scope. The unit pattern consists of twenty syllables, neither more nor less, sharply divided to the ear as well as to the eye into an even rhyme-pair of five-stress iambic lines. And the unit-pattern is given sharp definition; only occasionally are its outlines softened by a running-on of phrase from couplet to couplet, as with Chaucer and the Elizabethans on the one side or with Keats and William Morris on the other. If one casts one's eye down any page of Pope, one finds virtually every couplet stopped by a punctuation mark, which in most cases is semicolon or period; in an overwhelming majority of the couplets the first line also is stopped, usually by a comma. The pattern of the single line is thus defined almost as sharply as that of the couplet itself. It is no wonder that a reader accustomed to the metrical variety of the nineteenth-century poets with their intricate stanza-patterns, or to the deliberate blurring of the line divisions in the blank verse of Milton or of the mature Shakespeare, should chafe at the restrictions of Pope's couplet and should cry out on its monotony. Lowell, in his *Essay on Pope* (1871), speaks of "the lullaby seesaw of the couplet."

Dryden, and other seventeenth-century practitioners of the couplet, sought to avoid monotony by occasionally extending the ten-syllable line to a twelve-syllable Alexandrine, and by expanding the couplet into a triplet. With Dryden, particularly in his translation of Virgil, the triplet appears rather frequently. These devices Pope used sparingly. In his early translation of the first book of Statius there are twenty-two triplets in the 862 lines; they are frequent also in his paraphrases of Chaucer; but in the *Iliad* they would not average more than three or four to a book. In the final texts of the *Rape of the Lock, Eloisa,* the *Essay on Man, Dr. Arbuthnot,* and the *Dunciad* the triplet is not used at all; in the less highly wrought of his Horatian satires it is used sparingly. The Alexandrine and the triplet were apparently for Pope's mature taste too obvious a variation, too disturbing a departure from the discipline of his chosen form. His disapproval of the Alexandrine is expressed, and its quality illustrated, in a couplet of that section of the *Essay on Criticism* which deals with "numbers":

> A needless *Alexandrine* ends the song,
> That like a wounded snake, drags its slow length along.
>
> (356-7)

But variety and monotony are, like freedom and restriction, terms of relative significance. The manifold restrictions of civilized society make possible a richer freedom of action, at least for the man of civilized tastes, than can be realized in the apparently freer life of a frontier community. An Alexander Selkirk, though monarch of all he surveys, will find monotony one of the major evils of his desert-island domain. This is even truer in the world of the artist. Our greatest poets and painters have not fretted at the narrow confines set for them by the media or accepted conditions of their art. They can be bounded

in a nutshell and still count themselves kings of infinite space. They may even glory in the nutshell,
and find in it the provocation of an infinite artistic
spaciousness. To those whose tempers incline to discipline and order rather than to revolt and escape, the
free verse, the grammarless sentences, and unlexical
diction of those more "emancipated" writers in prose
and in verse, who like to call themselves "modern,"
offend not so much by their lawlessness as by their
dreadful monotony.

And so for Pope, the poet of discipline, of civilization and urbanity, of that order which is heaven's
first law, the narrow confines of the heroic couplet
gave adequate scope for an amazing variety of musical
effects. For his verse is monotonous only to those who
have never tuned their ears to its subtle modulations.
The reader of poetry accustomed to a wider range of
variation may need to learn the art of reading such
verse as that of Dryden and Pope. It must be read,
first of all, with a certain stateliness and deliberation
of utterance; it is not to be hurried. Its prevailing
tempo is andante; its steps are those of the minuet. It
must be read, also, with single-eyed attention to the
logical value of its words and phrases; each syllable
must be given the weight, and no more than the
weight, appropriate to it from the logic of the context,
with total unconcern for the rhythmical pattern of
the iambic line. Of that the poet himself has taken
full care. Any artificial weighting beyond its logical
value, given to a syllable because of its place in the

pattern, will mar if not destroy the intended music of the line.

This caution against an exaggerated weighting is particularly necessary as regards the syllables which carry the rhyme. The very fact of the rhyme enforces them upon the attention; and they are further heightened by the immediately ensuing pause which normally concludes the line. The rhyming word is moreover usually a significant word, and so one which demands a considerable weight of utterance. But the temptation of the reader who has not adequately caught the music of the couplet, is to make the rhyming syllable the heaviest of the line, even though the eighth syllable, or the sixth, may be clearly of greater logical import. In the familiar line—

> Hope springs eternal in the human breast,

the words of weight are *Hope* and *eternal*; *breast* should receive less emphasis than *human*, for Pope is still mindful of the "lamb thy riot dooms to bleed to-day" in the immediately preceding lines. The rhyme-word *breast* has no more logical importance than *springs*, a word which in the verse-pattern fills the place of a normally unstressed syllable. In uttering the rhyme-word one should err on the side of a lowered, rather than a heightened, weight of stress. A disregard of this principle, and a consequent bearing down on the rhyme, will debase the most musical passages of Pope's verse into monotonous sing-song.

How great a musical variety Pope could achieve within the nutshell limits of a single form may be

illustrated from two imaginary death-bed scenes; the
first is from *Eloisa to Abelard*:

> Ah no—in sacred vestments may'st thou stand,
> The hallow'd taper trembling in thy hand,
> Present the Cross before my lifted eye,
> Teach me at once, and learn of me to die.
> Ah then, thy once-lov'd *Eloisa* see!
> It will be then no crime to gaze on me.
> See from my cheek the transient roses fly!
> See the last sparkle languish in my eye!
> 'Til ev'ry motion, pulse, and breath be o'er;
> And ev'n my *Abelard* be lov'd no more.   (325-34)

The second is from the close of the first *Moral Essay*:

> "Odious! in woollen! 'twould a Saint provoke,"
> (Were the last words that poor Narcissa spoke)
> "No, let a charming Chintz, and Brussels lace
> Wrap my cold limbs, and shade my lifeless face:
> One would not, sure, be frightful when one's dead—
> And—Betty—give this Cheek a little Red."   (246-51)

The modulation of these passages is as different as
their sharply contrasted tone and temper.

The varying modulations of Pope's metric may be
considered first as they appear in the handling of the
single line. Within the line there are three principal
sources of variation: the treatment of pauses, the disposition of light and heavy syllables, and, subtlest in
its nature and therefore difficult to analyze, the tone-
quality of the vowel and consonant sounds which
make the phonetic texture of the line. Of these sources
of variety Pope was clearly conscious of the first and
the last; though he does not in his own discussions of
the matter explicitly mention the second, it is no
less important.

In a letter to his friend and early mentor Walsh, to which Pope has given the date October 22, 1706,[6] he discusses somewhat pedantically the theory of pauses and their variation. The normal line is to be read with an appreciable cæsura, which most often follows either the fourth or the fifth syllable. But the pause frequently follows the second syllable or the sixth, and it may follow any syllable except the first and the ninth. It was Pope's theory, set forth in the letter to Walsh—a theory not, however, always observed in his practice—that no pause should be "continued above three lines together." By this shifting pause the line is broken into two usually unequal members. Almost equally important is the duration of the pause, determined, as are all the modulations of Pope's verse, by the logic of the context. The pause may be of sufficient logical import to demand a mark of punctuation:

> Smooth flow the waves, the zephyrs gently play,
> *Belinda* smil'd, and all the world was gay.
>
> (*Rape of the Lock*, II, 51-2)

Here there is a fairly heavy cæsura after *waves*, and one not quite so heavy after *smil'd*. In the following couplet, a few lines later in the same passage from the *Rape of the Lock*, there is in the first line an all-but-imperceptible pause after the fourth syllable, and a slightly heavier pause after the fifth syllable of the second line:

> Soft o'er the shrouds aerial whispers breath,
> That seem'd but zephyrs to the train beneath. (II, 57-8)

Sometimes the line moves to its end with no pause at all, as in—

> Thin glitt'ring textures of the filmy dew.   (II, 64)

or—

> He summons strait his Denizens of air.   (II, 55)

Sometimes the single pause is multiplied to two or three, or even four, as in the highly colloquial opening lines of the *Epistle to Dr. Arbuthnot*:

> Shut, shut the door, good John! fatigu'd, I said,
> Tye up the knocker, say I'm sick, I'm dead.
> The Dog-star rages! nay 'tis past a doubt,
> All Bedlam, or Parnassus, is let out:
> Fire in each eye, and papers in each hand,
> They rave, recite, and madden round the land.

More important in the technique of Pope's couplet than the varying position and duration of the cæsural pause, is the varying disposition of heavy syllables and light. Here again the sole criterion for analysis is the normal accentuation of the word, and the logical importance of each word in its context. The basic rhythmical pattern consists of a regular alternation of light syllables and heavy, and of heavy syllables of approximately equal weight. It is perfectly exemplified in—

> And bid alternate passions fall and rise.
>   (*Essay on Criticism*, 375)

Such a perfect equality of syllables as this is not common. Even in lines where there are five heavy syllables in unbroken alternation, some of the heavy syllables are likely to have greater weight than others.

The most obvious variation of the basic line, freely used by Pope as by all other writers of iambic pentameter, is the shifting of the first stress, as in the line—

> Soft is the strain when *Zephyr* gently blows
>> (*Essay on Criticism*, 366)

So familiar is this variation, that such a line is almost as normal as the one previously quoted. Here again there are five heavy syllables, though the first three are appreciably heavier than the last two. If transposition of the stressed and unstressed syllables of the first foot is very common, similar transposition after a pause within the line, so common in Milton, is rare.

But every line does not contain five heavy syllables. One of the beats of the basic rhythm may coincide with a word of no logical weight whatsoever. If we follow the principle of giving to a syllable only the weight justified by its significance, one of the five stresses will be completely suppressed. To such a syllable no artificial weight should be given merely because of its place in the metrical pattern. The stress most often suppressed is the third. If suppression of the third stress is combined with a heavy pause after the fifth syllable, the result is a balanced line, such as—

> Now burns with glory, and then melts with love
>> (*Essay on Criticism*, 377)

If the cæsura is differently placed, a totally different modulation results:

> No more—but hasten to thy tasks at home.
>> (*Iliad*, VI, 632)

Suppression of the fourth stress is illustrated by the following lines:

> His purple pinions opening to the sun,
>> (*Rape of the Lock*, II, 71)

> The spider's touch, how exquisitely fine!
>> (*Essay on Man*, I, 217)

In the following lines the second stress is suppressed:

> Superior by the head, was *Ariel* plac'd,
>> (*Rape of the Lock*, II, 70)

> All Nature is but Art, unknown to thee;
>> (*Essay on Man*, I, 289)

One may stop to notice that these two lines, though accentually identical, have a very different modulation because of the different handling of the cæsura. In the first there is a heavy pause after the sixth syllable; in the second there is a very light pause after the third. Total suppression of the fifth stress, which carries the rhyme, is not possible; but the stress may be a very light one as in the line:

> And faith, our early immortality!
>> (*Eloisa*, 300)

where the third stress also is very light. The suppression of the first stress, if not otherwise compensated for, would result in a line beginning with three light syllables, which would too seriously blur the pattern. But not infrequent is the line which begins with two light syllables followed by two heavy ones, the weight of the second foot compensating the lightness of the first, as in—

> And the World's victor stood subdu'd by Sound
>> (*Essay on Criticism*, 381)

or in the following line, where a slight stress is given
to the first syllable, with much heavier weight on
the third and fourth:

> All this dread ORDER break—for whom? for thee?
>
> *(Essay on Man, I, 257)*

A very light line results from the suppression of both
the second and the fourth stresses:

> This Nymph, to the destruction of mankind
>
> *(Rape of the Lock, II, 19)*

If the normal line may be lightened by the suppression of one, or even of two, stresses, it may also be
given greater weight by the presence of more than the
normal number of heavy syllables. This metrical device is one of those which Pope deliberately exemplifies in the familiar passage of the *Essay on
Criticism* where, as sheer *tour de force*, he puts his
Pegasus through his metrical paces:

> When *Ajax* strives some rock's vast weight to throw,
> The line too labours, and the words move slow.
>
> *(Essay on Criticism, 370-1)*

In the first line of this couplet there are six unmistakably heavy syllables, and the second syllable of
Ajax and the word *some* are only relatively light; in
the second there are also six heavy syllables, but they
are divided into two balanced groups of three each at
the beginning and end of the line, with almost complete suppression of the third normal stress, which
coincides with *and*, a syllable only very slightly
heavier than those that precede and follow. The
different modulation of these lines results in part from

the disposition of the heavy syllables, in part from the treatment of the pause; the first line has a light pause after the fourth syllable, the second a heavier pause after the fifth.

Similar in modulation, though appreciably different in effect, is the line which contains five heavy syllables but with suppression of one of the normal stresses:

Thin glitt'ring textures of the filmy dew
(*Rape of the Lock*, II, 64)

Who heaves old Ocean, and who wings the storms
(*Essay on Man*, I, 158)

The number of heavy syllables may even be as many as seven, as in the following lines which are far removed from the basic pattern:

Beast, bird, fish, insect, what no eye can see
(*Essay on Man*, I, 239)

The hoarse, rough verse should like the torrent roar
(*Essay on Criticism*, 369)

We may distinguish, then, on the basis of the weight of syllables, three types of line, each with a variety of sub-types. There is the normal line with five heavy syllables—though not of uniform weight—disposed in regular alternation with light syllables, or with transposition in the first foot. There is the lightened line, with less than five heavy syllables and suppression of one of the normal stresses. There is the weighted line, with more than five heavy syllables, or with five heavy syllables and suppression of one of the normal stresses. The metrical effect of any passage will vary with the relative frequency of these three types.[7]

The various weighting of the syllables combined
with the various disposition and duration of pauses
makes possible an endless variety of modulation. As
important as these sources of variety, probably of
even greater importance, is the varying texture of the
line which results from the tone-quality of the
phonetic elements which make up its words—the
sequence of the vowels, the clash and harmony of the
consonants. Formal analysis of these subtle and com-
plex effects is difficult, and adequate analysis is impossible. Of this element of his art Pope was keenly
aware:

> There is a sweetness, that is the distinguishing char-
> acter of pastoral versification. The fourth and fifth
> syllables, and the last but two, are chiefly to be
> minded; and one must tune each line over in one's
> head, to try whether they go right or not. (Spence,
> p. 312)

The fourth and fifth syllables are of importance presumably because they most frequently precede the
cæsura; precisely why Pope regarded the eighth
syllable as of crucial consequence, I cannot explain.
How successfully he tuned his lines over in his head
needs no demonstration to any reader who will listen
to them with similar attention. Of all his couplets the
one which, he declared, best pleased his ear is:[8]

> Lo! where Mæotis sleeps, and hardly flows
> The freezing Tanais thro' a waste of snows.
> (*Dunciad*, III, 87-8)

One may notice that the long vowel of the rhyme-
words is anticipated in *Lo* and *Mæotis*, that the long

vowel of *freezing* echoes that of *sleeps*, that *s* and *z* sounds occur nine times in the two lines, and that *l* and *r* recur frequently (four times in combination with a breathed fricative). So much one can analyze; but such analysis does not in itself account for the exquisite music of the lines.

Another couplet of exceptional beauty is:

> The spider's touch, how exquisitely fine!
> Feels at each thread, and lives along the line.
>
> (*Essay on Man*, I, 217-18)

Here again the diphthong of the rhyme-words is anticipated in the stressed syllable of *spider's*; the delicacy of the spider's artistry is fittingly symbolized by the recurrence of the close short *i* sounds, the corresponding close long vowels of *feels* and *each*, and the half-close short *e* sounds of *ex-* and *thread*. These close vowels contrast with the more open vowel of *touch* and the open resonance of *along*.

So far we have been concerned with the individual line and with the couplet. While it is true that, formally considered, the couplet—usually closed with a logical pause so heavy that the punctuation demands at least a comma, and more often semicolon or full stop—is Pope's metrical unit, that is not the whole of the story. When Pope's metrical art is at its best, his couplets do not merely follow one upon another's heels. They group themselves into the larger unit of the verse-paragraph, the group being held together both by the logic of the sense and by the cadences of the modulation. This is particularly true of his more impassioned poetry—the elevated elo-

quence of the *Essay on Man* or the intense scorn of his
great satire. Of the twenty-two lines which paint the
satiric portrait of "Atticus," all but one are closed
with a mark of punctuation; of the couplets all but
one close with a pause which requires colon or semicolon. But the whole passage is grammatically a single
sentence, and this grammatical suspension welds
each couplet into the next, and the eleven couplets
into a unified musical movement. The portrait of
"Sporus" is disposed into a number of sentences, but
the sense of each sentence builds so closely on that of
the preceding sentence that a perfect unity of substance reflects itself in a unified system of cadences.

   Or we may take the following passage from near the
end of the first epistle of the *Essay on Man*:

> All are but parts of one stupendous whole,
> Whose body Nature is, and God the soul;
> That, chang'd thro' all, and yet in all the same;
> Great in the earth, as in th' æthereal frame;
> Warms in the sun, refreshes in the breeze,
> Glows in the stars, and blossoms in the trees,
> Lives thro' all life, extends thro' all extent,
> Spreads undivided, operates unspent;
> Breathes in our soul, informs our mortal part,
> As full, as perfect, in a hair as heart:
> As full, as perfect, in vile Man that mourns,
> As the rapt Seraph that adores and burns:
> To him no high, no low, no great, no small;
> He fills, he bounds, connects, and equals all.   (267-80)

Here, though every line is end-stopped, the seven
couplets compose a single sentence, with a complete
unity of meaning clearly pointed by the identity of the
first and last words of the passage—the word *all*,

which occurs also twice in the third line and twice in the seventh, and becomes the motivating theme of the whole. The length of this passage is exactly that of a sonnet. The next paragraph, which concludes the epistle, is also fourteen lines in length:

> Cease then, nor ORDER Imperfection name:
> Our proper bliss depends on what we blame.
> Know thy own point: This kind, this due degree
> Of blindness, weakness, Heav'n bestows on thee.
> Submit.—In this, or any other sphere,
> Secure to be as blest as thou canst bear:
> Safe in the hand of one disposing Pow'r,
> Or in the natal, or the mortal hour.
> All Nature is but Art, unknown to thee;
> All Chance, Direction, which thou canst not see;
> All Discord, Harmony not understood;
> All partial Evil, universal Good:
> And, spite of Pride, in erring Reason's spite,
> One truth is clear, WHATEVER IS, IS RIGHT.

Though, as printed, this passage falls into five sentences, the first eight lines develop a single aspect of the thought, and the following six have a unity sharply marked by parallelism of phrase and the fourfold repetition of a single word—again the word *all*. The opposition of the eight lines and the six gives to this passage an even greater resemblance to the sonnet. The "poor Indian" passage (I, 99-112) is also of fourteen lines, broken now into ten and four.

I do not for a moment suppose that this analogy with the sonnet was consciously in Pope's mind, for Pope and his generation were not much given to unlocking their hearts with this particular key; but it is none the less a fact that passages of elevated feeling

tend to approximate this limit. In the first epistle of
the *Essay on Man*, I count five such passages of
exactly fourteen lines, and others of twelve lines or
sixteen. Verse-paragraphs of twelve, fourteen, or sixteen lines abound in *Eloisa to Abelard*. The very moving passage which begins—"How happy is the blame-
less Vestal's lot!" (*Eloisa* 207-22)—is of sixteen lines.
In the following passage of equally lyric quality the
number is just fourteen, broken into two quatrains
and a sestet:

> What scenes appear where'er I turn my view,
> The dear Ideas, where I fly, pursue,
> Rise in the grove, before the altar rise,
> Stain all my soul, and wanton in my eyes.
> I waste the Matin lamp in sighs for thee,
> Thy image steals between my God and me,
> Thy voice I seem in ev'ry hymn to hear,
> With every bead I drop too soft a tear.
> When from the Censer clouds of fragrance roll,
> And swelling organs lift the rising soul,
> One thought of thee puts all the pomp to flight,
> Priests, Tapers, Temples, swim before my sight:
> In seas of flame my plunging soul is drowned,
> While Altars blaze, and Angels tremble round. (263-76)

Though Pope was quite regardless of the sonnet form
as such, his artistic instinct seems to have led him to
flights of song which have a similar extent and a
similar unity of movement.

By varying the position and duration of his pauses,
by various weighting or lightening of his syllables, by
an exquisitely fine ear for the sequence of tones in the
phonetic texture of his verse, Pope has given to his
couplets an amazing variety of musical effects, in-

finite metrical riches within the little room of twenty syllables. But because the limits of the pattern are narrow, the variations are of a delicate subtlety which demands in the reader a corresponding niceness of musical perception. He has not only wrought marvels with the couplet, but has built his couplets up into the larger unity of the verse-paragraph, with a power of sustained harmony possible only to our greater poetic artists.

III

COOL PASTORALS

THE canons of poetic art set forth in the *Essay on Criticism* are essentially those which we sum up in the word neo-classical. Pope's neo-classicism is, to be sure, of the more liberal sort, like that of Boileau, whose *Art Poétique* was his chief exemplar; but his critical principles are those which he derived from "all the best critics" whom he devoured so hungrily in those years of voracious reading at Binfield, and the "best critics" were for the most part those of seventeenth-century France. He was later to liberalize his neo-classicism much further in the Prefaces to Homer and to Shakespeare; and the best of his poetry was to attain a degree of excellence which lies beyond any such restricting label as "neo-classical."

It is but natural, however, that his earliest original compositions should, like his early formulation of critical theories, have kept to the path which the "best critics" had pointed out to him. As a precocious little boy of twelve, he had not been afraid to tackle the very highest peaks of Helicon and to try his hand at what his critics assured him were the most exalted of all poetical forms, tragedy and the heroic epic. By the time that he was sixteen he had learned humility. He was now content to commence poet with one of the "lower" orders of poetry, and to pipe on the slender reed of the pastoral—as Virgil had begun eighteen hundred years before him.

His four pastorals of the four seasons, with their well-worn conventions, the brilliant *tour de force* of his "sacred eclogue," the *Messiah*, and the coolly idyllic *Windsor Forest* are completely within the neo-classical pattern. These poems have the quality of exquisite music and an unmistakable competence in literary craftsmanship—and very little more. There is in them no hint of the poetical power that was presently to manifest itself in the extended *Rape of the Lock*, or of the splendid energy which was to inform the *Dunciad* and the *Epistle to Dr. Arbuthnot*.

I

On April 20, 1706, a month before young Mr. Pope had attained his eighteenth birthday, Jacob Tonson, one of the leading booksellers of London, addressed to him a most flattering letter:

> Sir,—I have lately seen a Pastoral of yours in Mr. Walsh's and Mr. Congreve's hands, which is extremely fine, and is generally approved of by the best judges in poetry. I remember I have formerly seen you at my shop, and am sorry I did not improve my acquaintance with you. If you design your poem for the press, no person shall be more careful in the printing of it, nor no one can give greater encouragement to it than, sir, your, &c
>
> JACOB TONSON [1]

The *Pastorals* had been for some time in the hands of Mr. Walsh and Mr. Congreve, and of other men of letters who had taken up and made much of the pre-

cocious boy. Though Pope is notoriously careless—
hostile critics have said mendacious—about dates, he
is at least consistent in his assertions that the *Pastorals* were written in 1704, "at the age of sixteen,"
and there seems to be no reason to doubt the essential
truth of the assertion.

Though Jacob Tonson had solicited the privilege
of publishing Pope's *Pastorals* in April 1706, three
years were to elapse before the actual publication. In
May, 1709, appeared a stout octavo volume of over
650 pages[2] with the title:

> Poetical Miscellanies: The Sixth Part. Containing a
> Collection of Original Poems, With Several New
> Translations.—By the most Eminent Hands.—
> London, Printed for Jacob Tonson, within Grays-
> Inn Gate, next Grays-Inn Lane. 1709.—Where you
> may have the Five former Parts.[3]

Pope had contributed to these *Miscellanies* not only
"Original Poems" but "Several New Translations."
On pages 177-224 is printed *January and May*, and on
pages 301-323, "The Episode of Sarpedon, Translated from the Twelfth and Sixteenth Books of
Homer's Iliads." At the very end of the volume are
found the *Pastorals*, set off with a separate title page:

> Pastorals. By Mr. Alexander Pope.—
> London, Printed in the Year, 1709.

When Pope's *Pastorals* were reprinted in the collected works of 1717, they were accompanied by a
prefatory "Discourse on Pastoral Poetry," which, so
the poet assures us, was written at the same time as
the poems themselves. It is a graceful, but totally

unoriginal, digest of what all the "best critics" had to
say about the nature of the Pastoral and the "rules"
which the bucolic poet should follow. All of its ideas,
and many of its phrases, come from a few readily
accessible sources: from the "Preface to the Pastorals" which the Rev. Knightly Chetwood had
written for Dryden's translation of Virgil (1697) and
from Dryden's own "Dedication" to Lord Clifford,
from Fontenelle's "Discourse of Pastorals," and from
Rapin's *De Carmine Pastorali*, which Pope read in the
translation of Thomas Creech (1684).

It had been Pope's "design to comprize in this short
paper the substance of those numerous dissertations
the Criticks have made on the subject." The critics
are all agreed that the Pastoral belongs to the
literature of escape. The anonymous author of the
Guardian essays on this theme puts it thus:

> Pastoral Poetry not only amuses the Fancy the most
> delightfully, but is likewise more indebted to it than
> any other sort whatsoever. It transports us into a kind
> of *Fairy Land*, where our ears are soothed with the
> Melody of Birds, bleating Flocks, and purling Streams;
> our eyes enchanted with flowery Meadows and spring-
> ing Greens; we are laid under cool shades, and enter-
> tained with all the Sweets and Freshness of Nature. It
> is a Dream, 'tis a Vision, which we wish may be real,
> and we believe that it is true.[4]

And Pope says in his "Discourse":

> If we would copy Nature, it may be useful to take
> this consideration along with us, that pastoral is an
> image of what they call the Golden age. So that we are

not to describe our shepherds as shepherds at this day really are, but as they may be conceiv'd then to have been.[5]

And again:

The complete character of this poem consists in simplicity, brevity, and delicacy; the two first of which render an eclogue natural, and the last delightful.

Theocritus and Virgil are, of course, "the only undisputed authors of Pastoral"; but there was room for dispute as to which of these two authors, the original master or the pupil, has precedence. There is the same antithesis as between Homer and Virgil in the epic: "*Theocritus* excells all others in nature and simplicity"; "*Virgil* who copies *Theocritus*, refines upon his original: and in all points where Judgment has the principal part, is much superior to his master." And so the critics, while praising both poets, side with one or the other as their allegiance is chiefly to Nature or to Art. For Fontenelle, Virgil errs by being frequently too elevated, too sophisticated. For Rapin, Theocritus is too diffuse, and sometimes "keeps too close to the *Clown*, and is rustick and uncouth."

Our English Spenser, with his "country phrases" and his "Tetrastic" stanza is too uncouth. "As there is a difference betwixt simplicity and rusticity, so the expression of simple thoughts should be plain, but not clownish." Pope, though he has here as elsewhere in his critical theories tried to reconcile the warring camps, is clearly on the side of Virgil rather than of

Theocritus—and Spenser. His own pastorals are polite, whereas those of Ambrose Philips are clownishly rustic. Pope's practice, as well as his theory, is in accord with the advice of Rapin:

> For what is more hard than to be always in the *Country*, and yet never to be *Clownish*? to sing of *mean*, and trivial matters, yet not *trivially*, and *meanly*? to pipe on a *slender* Reed, and yet keep the sound from being *harsh*, and *squeaking*? to make every thing *sweet*, yet never satiate?[6]

To expect, then, that Pope's *Pastorals* shall present with even the most distant approach to realism the actual life of the English peasantry, to look in them for the virtues of Gay's *Shepherd's Week* or of Wordsworth's *Michael*, is to read them in a spirit totally alien to that in which their author writ. Nor even within the frame of his convention does the young Pope make any claim to originality. The prefatory "Discourse" ends with this disclaimer:

> But after all, if they have any merit, it is to be attributed to some good old Authors, whose works as I had leisure to study, so I hope I have not wanted care to imitate.

That Pope has not "wanted care to imitate" becomes unmistakably plain, when one consults the notes to the Elwin-Courthope edition. Most often the debt is to Virgil (usually in Dryden's rendering), but among the "good old Authors" are included Sidney, Spenser, Milton's Minor Poems, Waller, Dryden, Congreve, and (in translation) Theocritus and Moschus. Pope's honey is gathered from all the flowers of poetry.

Dr. Johnson in his Life of Pope sums up the matter thus:

> To charge these *Pastorals* with want of invention is to require what was never intended. The imitations are so ambitiously frequent that the writer evidently means rather to shew his literature than his wit. It is surely sufficient for an author of sixteen, not only to be able to copy the poems of antiquity with judicious selection, but to have obtained sufficient power of language and skill in metre to exhibit a series of versification, which had in English poetry no precedent, nor has since had an imitation.

What is memorable in Pope's *Pastorals* is not their substance. The Golden Age which they profess to imitate, with its pretty artifice of simplicity, provides no alluring avenue of escape for us today. Neither, for that matter, does the pastoral world of Virgil and his Greek originals. What we value in the eclogues of Virgil is their exquisite rightness and grace of utterance. And so with Pope. Like the bee in Swift's apologue, he has gathered his honey from the flowers; all that is his own is voice and wings. Rapin had said:

> For there is no part of *Poetry* that requires more spirit, for if any part is not close and well compacted the whole Fabrick will be ruin'd, and the matter, in it self humble, must creep; unless it is held up by the strength and vigor of the *Expression*.[7]

And Pope, looking back in his later years at these boyhood productions, could say:

> Notwithstanding the early time of their production, the Author esteem'd these as the most correct in the versification, and musical in the numbers, of all his works. The reason for his labouring them into so much

> softness, was, that this sort of poetry derives almost
> its whole beauty from a natural ease of thought and
> smoothness of verse; whereas that of most other kinds
> consists in the Strength and fulness of both.[8]

Most musical of the four, I think, is *Autumn*, with
its slightly varied recurring refrains. The beginning
of Ægon's song has delicate grace of imagery as well
as music:

> Resound, ye hills, resound my mournful strain!
> Of perjur'd *Doris*, dying I complain!
> Here where the mountains, les'ning as they rise,
> Lose the low vales, and steal into the skies.
> While lab'ring Oxen, spent with toil and heat,
> In their loose traces from the field retreat;
> While curling smoaks from village-tops are seen,
> And the fleet shades glide o'er the dusky green.

To Joseph Warton it seemed "something strange, that
in the pastorals of a young poet there should not be
found a single rural image that is new."[9] The rural
images of these lines are not new, perhaps, but the
young poet has made of them the substance of very
graceful poetry.

II

On May 14, 1712, the *Spectator* (No. 378) is devoted
to "Messiah: A Sacred Eclogue," but the author's
name is not revealed. Mr. Spectator (who is here
Richard Steele) merely tells his readers that it is
"written by a great genius, a friend of mine in the
country, who is not ashamed to employ his wit in the
praise of his Maker." Exactly six months later, on
November 12, 1712 (No. 534), Mr. Spectator reveals
that "that excellent piece is Mr. Pope's." When it was

written we have no means of discovering. One may
guess that had it been written very long before its
publication in the *Spectator* it would have been included in the *Miscellanies* of Tonson, or in Lintot's
Miscellany, which was published a week later than
the *Messiah*, but which must have been made up
some time earlier.

Stricter critics of the neo-classic era were troubled
because one of Virgil's eclogues was not properly a
pastoral. Eclogue IV, instead of looking back wist-
fully to a vanished golden age of pastoral tranquillity,
foretells in poetry exalted to the measure of its high
theme a new golden age under the great Augustus,
which is to be ushered in by the birth of a marvelous
boy, probably son to C. Asinius Pollio, consul in
40 B.C., to whom the eclogue is addressed. The high
prophetic strains of this eclogue are so suggestive of
the Messianic prophecies of Isaiah, that through
many Christian centuries Virgil was accorded a place
in men's thought only a little lower than the Hebrew
prophets.

Pope in his *Messiah* has made what might be called
a poetic "harmony" of Virgil and Isaiah. In the
Spectator for May 14, 1712, where it was first printed,
the author described it as "A Sacred Eclogue, Composed of Several Passages of Isaiah the Prophet,
Written in imitation of Virgil's Pollio." The passages
from Isaiah were duly indicated in footnotes. When it
was reprinted in the collected Works of 1717 as one
of Pope's *Pastorals*, it was further annotated by
quotations from Virgil set alongside of the similar

verses in Isaiah. In the accompanying "Advertise-ment," Pope explained his procedure. As Virgil had selected from the Sybilline books "such Ideas as best agreed with the nature of pastoral poetry, and dis-posed them in that manner which serv'd most to beautify his piece," so Pope has written an imitation of the "Pollio" by selecting images and ideas from Isaiah and from Virgil, "*tho' without admitting any thing of my own*." I have italicized the last phrase, because it seems to me to make clear that to the poet himself the *Messiah* was a work of ingenious literary craftsmanship rather than one dictated by deep re-ligious feeling. Pope has set himself a task, has de-vised rules for its accomplishment, and has punctili-ously observed the rules that he had devised. His invocation to the Seraph "who touch'd *Isaiah's* hallow'd lips with fire!" is but an artistic device, reminiscent, perhaps, of Milton's *Hymn on the Na-tivity*. The images and ideas of Isaiah which Pope has "selected" are, as his own annotations show, from widely scattered portions of the Biblical text. A dozen different chapters of Isaiah are laid under con-tribution. But though ideas and images are borrowed, the diction is completely changed. In his annotations Pope quotes the following sentences from Isaiah XI:

> The wolf shall dwell with the lamb, and the leopard shall lie down with the kid, and the calf and the young lion and the fatling together; and a little child shall lead them—And the lion shall eat straw like the ox. And the sucking child shall play on the hole of the asp, and the weaned child shall put his hand on the den of the cockatrice.

In Pope these verses become:

> The lambs with wolves shall graze the verdant mead,
> And boys in flow'ry bands the Tyger lead;
> The steer and lion at one crib shall meet.
>
> The smiling infant in his hand shall take
> The crested Basilisk and speckled snake;
> Pleas'd the green lustre of the scales survey,
> And with their forky tongue and pointless sting shall play.

Every one, I suppose, will agree that the Authorized Version, with its straightforward and homely diction and the unadorned simplicity of its images, is more moving in its sublimity than the elaborated images and the polished elegance of Pope. To Wordsworth and to many critics since his time the *Messiah* has been only a deplorable mistake. For the Rev. Whitwell Elwin this critical judgment was reinforced by a feeling that Pope is almost a blasphemer when he undertakes to elevate and improve Holy Writ. Such criticism results from substituting the critic's expectation for the author's intention. Pope undertook to improve not the Book of Isaiah but the "Pollio" of Virgil. He is writing in imitation of Virgil, and the poetic style is not Biblical but Virgilian. It is in imitation of the manner of Virgil that "and a little child shall lead them" has become—"And boys *in flow'ry bands* the Tyger lead." Pope is, as it were, giving us an English version of the eclogue that Virgil might have written, could he have drawn on Isaiah rather than, as Pope believed he had done, on the Sybilline prophecy. The *Messiah* was, Pope tells us, "written with this particular view, that the reader . . . might see how far the images and descriptions of the Prophet are superior to those of the Poet."

As the four earlier pastorals imitate the elegance of Virgil's lower style, the *Messiah* imitates his grander manner—*paulo maiora canamus*—and, so considered, it is a magnificent *tour de force*. And it is something more than this. The images of Isaiah have been so skillfully fitted into the pattern of Pope's mosaic, and have been set to so stately a music, that no sympathetic reader can fail to be moved by such grandiose lines as—

> Rise, crown'd with light, imperial *Salem* rise!
> Exalt thy tow'ry head, and lift thy eyes!
> See, a long race thy spacious courts adorn;
> See future sons, and daughters yet unborn,
> In crouding ranks on ev'ry side arise,
> Demanding life, impatient for the skies.

From these lines, and from those that follow, has been devised a familiar hymn, which has found and held a place in all the hymnals of the English-speaking world.

III

In the opening footnote to *Windsor Forest* in the collected edition of 1743, Pope has this to say about the composition of the poem:

> This Poem was written at two different times: the first part of it which relates to the country, in the year 1704, at the same time with the Pastorals: the latter part was not added till the year 1710, in which it was published.

In Warburton's edition of 1751 the date "1710" is corrected to read "1713"; but the note is otherwise unchanged.

At line 290 (wrongly numbered 288), "And add new lustre to her silver star," there is a further note:[10]

> All the lines that follow were not added to the poem
> till the year 1710. What immediately followed this,
> and made the Conclusion, were these:

> My humble Muse in unambitious strains
> Paints the green forests and the flow'ry plains;
> Where I obscurely pass my careless days,
> Pleas'd in the silent shade with empty praise,
> Enough for me that to the list'ning swains
> First in these fields I sung the sylvan strains.

The poem, as Pope printed it in 1713, is, then, a composite, or, more accurately, a sylvan poem of Pope's earliest years to which has been appended a poem in praise of the Peace of Utrecht. The poetic Judgment which was to guide Pope so beautifully through the delicate task of expanding the *Rape of the Lock* failed him, I think, in this instance. The resulting poem of 434 lines is, for one thing, too long for a sort of composition which has no sustaining fable or ordered argument. The grandiose lines—some of them very fine lines—spoken by Father Thames as he looks forward to his future commercial greatness when he—

> shall flow for all mankind,
> Whole nations enter with each swelling tyde,
> And Seas but join the regions they divide—

are in a very different tone from the "sylvan strains" of the unexpanded poem.

The shorter *Windsor Forest* has, too, a much greater measure of structural unity. After an introductory paragraph of invocation and of dedication to Lord Lansdowne, follow thirty-five lines (7-42) of generalized description of the Forest:

> Here waving groves a checquer'd scene display,
> And part admit, and part exclude the day;
> . . . .
> There, interspers'd in lawns and opening glades,
> Thin trees arise that shun each others shades.
> Here in full light the russet plains extend;
> There wrapt in clouds the blueish hills ascend:

Then, contrasted with the "Peace and Plenty" which "tell a *Stuart* reigns," follow fifty lines (43-92) which take us back to "ages past," when under the savage tyranny of the early Norman kings the Forest was a scene of desolation reserved for the sport of royal huntsmen. Next follow seventy lines (93-164) which show that the Forest is still, in each of the four seasons, a sportsman's paradise. There is in the autumn the shooting of partridges and of the "whirring Pheasant"—

> Ah! what avail his glossy, varying dyes,
> His purple crest, and scarlet-circled eyes,
> The vivid green his shining plumes unfold,
> His painted wings, and breast that flames with gold?

In the winter there is hunting of the hare and the shooting of woodcocks and plovers and of the "mounting Larks," who "fall, and leave their little lives in air." Spring brings the fishing season, and summer the coursing of the "fleet hart." The theme of hunting brings us, unfortunately, to Diana, who is of course the type of Queen Anne (a royal lady who in 1704 was a "bright Goddess" just under forty years of age!), and Diana introduces the dull story of the metamorphosis of the virgin nymph, Lodona. This is the sort of stuff which Addison in *Spectator* 523 branded as "downright puerility, and unpardonable in a poet that is past sixteen." If we may accept Pope's statement that the earlier part of *Windsor Forest* was written in 1704, he was just sixteen when he metamorphosed Lodona. From the River Loddon, we pass to the praises of the Thames (219-34). The mythological puerilities behind us, we come to the charming passage (235-58) in which for the first time the young poet shows something of his own life at Binfield on the borders of the Forest, a life of "successive study, exercise, and ease." Pope, all his soul possessed by the Sacred Nine, loves the Forest for itself and even more because its shade has been made venerable by Denham and by Cowley. They are gone, but Lord Lansdowne remains to "call the Muses to their ancient seats." The poem then concluded with the six lines quoted above on page 63 which bring it to a quiet close. The final line—

> First in these fields I sung the sylvan strains—

echoes the first line of the first *Pastoral*:

> First in these fields I try the sylvan strains.

Had not Virgil closed his *Georgics* with the first line of his *Eclogues*, modified only by the change of a single word?

For neo-classical criticism of the more authoritarian type the *Georgics* are the chief justification for that lower kind of poetry, the descriptive. There are in Pope's poem occasional echoes of Virgil's *Georgics*, as there are echoes of many other "good old Authors"; but its chief original is, of course, Denham's *Cooper's Hill*, the earliest important example of what Dr. Johnson denominates *"local poetry*, of which the fundamental subject is some particular landscape to be poetically described, with the addition of such embellishments as may be supplied by historical retrospection, or incidental meditation." Cooper's Hill is on the eastern edge of Windsor Forest, Pope's home at Binfield was on the western edge. From the top of the hill, Denham looks eastward to London and moralizes on the life of the city. In the opposite direction he looks towards Windsor Castle and reviews the great names which have been associated with its history. On a nearby hill is a ruined chapel that leads to a discussion of the Reformation, which despoiled the Church while purifying it. He looks down at the Thames and sings its praises, with animadversions on the glories of commerce. There is a royal hunting on the plain below, and a glance at Runnimede brings in the proper relation of subject and king. The description is only incidental to the moralizing. It is not an exciting poem, even less exciting, I think, than Pope's *Windsor Forest*. To it Pope owes very little beyond the suggestion. Until Pope expanded his original composition by the panegyric on

the Peace, there was much more of the Forest and
less of moralizing reflection than in *Cooper's Hill*.

Pope's method of expanding the poem was a very
simple one. Its six concluding lines were lopped off
and, with an added couplet about the blessings of
peace, were moved on to the end of the expanded
poem. To the praises of Denham and Cowley is
added a tribute to Surrey, "the Granville of a former
age," who was also a frequenter of the Forest. Granville is then invited to sing about the great names
associated with Windsor Castle: Edward III, Henry
VI, Edward IV, and in high Tory mood of the
calamities which followed on the execution of "sacred
Charles."

> At length great *Anna* said—Let discord cease!
> She said, the world obey'd, and all was Peace!

And in "that blest moment" Father Thames firmly
grasping his engraved urn, concludes the poem with a
highly wrought address to "sacred Peace" which is to
make him greater than all the famed rivers of the
globe, his estuary the home port of a world-wide commerce, which shall bind together the whole world in
peace and amity.

> Earth's distant ends our glory shall behold,
> And the new world launch forth to seek the old.
> Then ships of uncouth form shall stem the tyde,
> And feather'd people crowd my wealthy side,
> Whose naked youth and painted chiefs admire
> Our speech, our colour, and our strange attire!
> Oh stretch thy reign, fair Peace! from shore to shore,
> Till conquest cease, and slav'ry be no more:

The fine eloquence of the lines spoken by Father Thames was peculiarly acceptable to the Tories who, against bitter Whig opposition, were concluding the Treaty of Utrecht. On March 9, 1713, two days after *Windsor Forest* was published, Swift, greatest of all the Tories, wrote to Stella in his *Journal*: "Mr. Pope has published a fine poem, called Windsor Forest. Read it." It is Swift's first mention in any surviving document of the younger man who was very shortly, and for all the rest of his life, to become one of his dearest friends. It was doubtless the praise of the Peace which caught the attention of Swift. As the poem stands this is its chief note. The sylvan poem which in its graceful artifice, its cool absence of any emotion, is linked to the *Pastorals* has become merely a pedestal from which Father Thames utters his speech. I think it is a pity that Pope did not publish the original poem, as he might have done, in Lintot's *Miscellany* of 1712; and, if praise the Peace he must, do so in a poem of uniform tone and temper. *Windsor Forest*, as it stands, injures rather than helps his reputation. If it has some of the virtues, it also has most of the vices of the narrowly neo-classical poem. Hereafter Pope was to write with more poetic fire.

IV

THE MAZE OF FANCY

I

FOR over a century literary criticism has busied itself with speculation, necessarily fruitless, as to what might have happened if the young poet John Keats had not ceased to be before his pen had gleaned his teeming brain. Or what might have been, if Shelley's "fatal and perfidious bark" had not foundered in the Bay of Lerici? We shall never know. No literary historian is wise enough to guess the answer. There is another sort of literary might-have-been, however, which leads to speculation not quite so vain and unprofitable. When Shelley died, he was within a month of attaining his thirtieth birthday. If we may indulge in the crime of imaginary poeticide, and kill off Mr. Alexander Pope at precisely the same age, his demise will fall in April of 1718. What would have been the nature of his literary reputation had he died before reaching the age of thirty, is a question which can be answered with some degree of assurance. In the preceding June had appeared from the shop of Bernard Lintot, "between the Temple-Gates," two handsome volumes, issued both, it would seem, on the same day, June the third. One was Vol. III of the *Iliad*, containing Books IX-XII; the other bore the title: "The Works of Mr. Alexander Pope."

The poetry printed in this volume was an achievement brilliant enough to have insured the permanence of Pope's fame to future generations, if he had not lived to publish another line. His exquisite mastery of the music of verse is apparent on almost every page; within the restricted compass of the heroic couplet he has achieved an amazing variety of rhythm and of tonal effect. In substance, also, there is ample range— from the cool tranquillity of the *Pastorals* and *Windsor Forest* at one end of the volume to the glowing intensity of *Eloisa* at the other. The *Rape of the Lock*, that masterpiece supreme in its kind in the whole of European literature, shows his brilliant play of poetic fancy, that fancy which could dip in the richest tincture of the skies something so commonplace as a game of cards or the brewing of a pot of coffee. Both the *Rape* and the *Essay on Criticism* reveal his power of terse and witty epigram. The latest pieces in the 1717 collection, *Eloisa* and the *Unfortunate Lady*, are in substance, if not in execution, wholly romantic— medieval gloom, supernatural horror, pensive melancholy are there in abundance. A generation ago literary historians of the eighteenth century spent much of their time in hunting for so-called "precursors" of romanticism. Where a better precursor than Pope—if he had really died, as we are supposing, in the spring of 1718?

Of the more considerable pieces of the 1717 volume, the *Temple of Fame*, of which two editions had been published in 1715, is (with a certain irony) the one that contributes least to Pope's reputation. I find it

essentially a dull performance; but it is in its intention, at any rate, a further indication of Pope's
romantic leanings. Chaucer's tale of January and
May, and the Prologue of the Wife of Bath have,
particularly in Pope's versions of them, very little of
that glamour of romance which for the eighteenth
century and most of the nineteenth was implied by
the word medieval; but the elaborated allegory of the
House of Fame savours strongly of the "Gothick"
past. Pope's *Temple of Fame*, "written," so the half-
title of the 1717 volume informs us, "in the year
1711," is a very free reworking of the third book of
Chaucer's poem; Pope printed it with his own original
pieces, and not under the caption of "Translations."[1]
As he says in the "Advertisement," "The design is in
a manner entirely alter'd, the descriptions and most
of the particular thought my own."

One of the descriptions which is Pope's own is the
winterpiece of Nova Zembla:

> So *Zembla's* rocks (the beauteous work of frost)
> Rise white in air, and glitter o'er the coast;
> Pale suns, unfelt, at distance roll away,
> And on th' impassive ice the lightnings play;
> Eternal snows the growing mass supply,
> Till the bright mountains prop th' incumbent sky:
> As *Atlas* fix'd, each hoary pile appears,
> The gather'd winter of a thousand years.

These lines are fine enough to redeem a poem much
duller than the *Temple of Fame*; the first two couplets
are, I think, as beautiful as any that Pope ever wrote.
On this passage Pope supplied in the editions of 1715[2]

a note which is in effect an apology for the romantic improbability of his poem:

> Tho' a strict Verisimilitude be not requir'd in the Descriptions of this visionary and allegorical kind of Poetry, which admits of every wild Object that Fancy may present in a Dream, and where it is sufficient if the moral Meaning atone for the Improbability: Yet Men are naturally so desirous of Truth, that a Reader is generally pleas'd, in such a case, with some Excuse or Allusion that seems to reconcile the Description to Probability and Nature. The Simile here is of that sort, and renders it not wholly unlikely that a Rock of Ice should remain for ever, by mentioning something like it in the Northern Regions, agreeing with the Accounts of our modern Travellers.

II

The *Rape of the Lock* contains such infinite riches of poetic fancy within the short compass of its five cantos, that one is in danger of forgetting that its playful machinery of Ariel and his sylphs and the descent to the Cave of Spleen put it also into the "visionary and allegorical kind of poetry" of which "strict verisimilitude" is not required. If, on the one hand, it puts us quite at our ease in the drawing rooms of Hampton Court, it also takes us into Fairy Land— or more accurately annexes Fairy Land to the demesnes of Hampton Court. In the sum total of this, the most delicious of "heroi-comical" poems, one of the essential ingredients is sheer romantic fancy. It is this ingredient, I think, which raises it so far above the brilliant play of wit into the regions of great poetry.

When, in the final couplet of the poem, Pope wrote that—

> This Lock, the Muse shall consecrate to fame,
> And 'midst the stars inscribe *Belinda*'s name,

he uttered a prophecy which was to be abundantly verified. Mistress Arabella Fermor, and that greatly daring *beau*, Lord Petre, the severed lock and the resulting minor quarrel between the two families, are, after two centuries and more, familiar to every reader of English poetry. If Mr. John Caryll had never suggested to Pope that a graceful poem, which should play lightly with the whole affair, might serve to lay this teapot-tempest within that set of Roman Catholic families with which the Carylls and the Popes were associated, and so "laugh them together again," no one would ever have heard of the matter— *carent quia vate sacro.*

The first *Rape of the Lock*, a poem of 334 lines in two cantos, was printed without the author's name, and with no hint as to the identity of its heroine, as the last piece in Lintot's *Miscellany*, which appeared on May 20, 1712. It had been written, so Pope tells us, "in less than a fortnight's time" in the preceding year. Pope told Spence that the poem "was well received, and had its effect in the two families"; but its publication led to new embroilments. Though no names were given, every one within Mrs. Fermor's social set must have recognized the episode at first sight. Was it quite becoming that the personal adventures of a young lady should be so blazoned to the world, and with a number of rather equivocal lines? Nor did Sir

George Brown like his fictitious name of Sir Plume. Six months after the poem's publication, Pope wrote on November 8, 1712 to the younger Caryll: "Sir Plume blusters, I hear; nay the celebrated lady herself is offended."

The *Rape of the Lock* in its earlier version is a brilliant and delicious piece of playful fancy. Pope might well have been content to let it stand. Just when it occurred to him to revise his *jeu d'esprit* into the full stature of a mock epic, we do not know. The additions were completed, or nearly so, when on December 15, 1713, Pope wrote from Binfield to Mr. Caryll:

> I have been employed, since my being here in the country, in finishing the additions to the Rape of the Lock, a part of which I remember I showed you. I have some thoughts of dedicating that poem to Mrs. Fermor by name, as a piece of justice in return to (*sic*) the wrong interpretations she has suffered under on the score of that piece.

And again on January 9, 1714:

> As to the Rape of the Lock, I believe I have managed the dedication so nicely that it can neither hurt the lady nor the author. I writ it very lately, and upon great deliberation. The young lady approves of it, and the best advice in the kingdom, of the men of sense, has been made use of in it, even to the Treasurer's [Lord Oxford]. A preface which salved the lady's honour, without affixing her name, was also prepared, but by herself superseded in favour of the dedication.[3] Not but that, after all, fools will talk, and fools will hear them.

If Pope had had "the best advice in the kingdom" about the dedication, he had also sought advice about the "machinery" which he added to the poem. As Pope told Spence (p. 195), "the scheme of adding it was much liked and approved of by several of my friends, and particularly by Dr. Garth; who, as he was one of the best natured men in the world, was very fond of it." Addison, on the other hand, whose acquaintance Pope first made in this very year of 1713, advised against any alteration of what was already "a delicious little thing, and, as he expressed it, *merum sal.*"[4]

Fortunately it was Garth's advice and not Addison's that Pope chose to follow. Pope may well have thought that Garth was particularly competent to advise on such a matter; for Garth was the author of a highly successful mock epic. The *Dispensary*, first published in 1699, recounts in six heroic cantos the quarrels which ensued when the College of Physicians undertook to prepare and deliver medicines to the poor at low and reasonable rates, to the great scandal of the apothecaries. Though very acceptable to contemporary readers who knew of the quarrel and could identify the personalities, the *Dispensary*, despite the nervous vigour of its couplets, is for us today rather dull reading. Pope, doubtless, read it with keen zest. Garth had been one of those elder men of letters who early took the youthful Pope under their care. The Huntington Library has a copy of the Sixth Edition of the *Dispensary*, "With several Descriptions and Episodes never before Printed. London, Printed: And Sold by *John Nutt*, near *Stationers-Hall*. 1706.", which is inscribed in a fine hand: "E Libris Alex:

Pope. 1706." Throughout the volume are brief marginal annotations, unmistakably in Pope's hand, which consist chiefly in identifications of the persons of the poem. In the Preface to this edition Garth confesses that he has "imitated the *Lutrin* of Monsieur Boileau."

Boileau's *Lutrin*, of which the first four cantos were published in 1674, with the fifth and sixth following in 1683,[5] is the point of departure for a new type of burlesque poem. Such burlesques as Scarron's *Virgile Travesti* make merry with heroic figures, who are made to speak and act like the most vulgar of ordinary mortals. It was Boileau's method, new for his generation, to do what Chaucer had done in the *Nun's Priest's Tale*, to clothe an insignificant action and mean personages in the trappings of an heroic poem. In an often quoted sentence of the "Avis au Lecteur" in the edition of 1674, Boileau explains his procedure:

> C'est un burlesque nouveau, dont je me suis avisé en notre langue; car, au lieu que dans l'autre burlesque Didon et Énée parloient comme des harengères et des crocheteurs, dans celui-ci une horlogère et un horloger parlent comme Didon et Énée.

Ozell, whose translation of the *Lutrin* published in 1708 with a prefatory letter by N. Rowe was very probably read by Pope, in his Dedication to Lord Halifax puts the matter thus:

> If I distinguish right, there are two sorts of *Burlesque*; the first where things of mean Figure and Slight Concern appear in all the Pomp and Bustle of an *Epic* Poem; such is this of the *Lutrin*. The second sort is where Great Events are made Ridiculous by

the meanness of the Character, and the oddness of the
Numbers, such is the *Hudibras* of our excellent *Butler*.

In the *Lutrin* the "pomp and bustle of an epic poem"
are bestowed upon a quarrel among the clergy of a
Paris church as to the placing of a new lectern.

To Boileau, and his imitator, Dr. Garth, Pope owes,
no doubt, the general idea of this newer sort of "heroi-
comical poem"; but beyond this his obligations are
negligible. To the *Secchia Rapita* of Tassoni (1622)
Pope owes nothing but his title; the "raped bucket"
has become the raped lock of hair. Tassoni's *Secchia*
is *poema eroicomico* of a different order.[6]

Neither the *Lutrin* nor the *Dispensary* brings upon
the field of its action the gods and goddesses of
Olympus. The supernatural "machinery," indispensable to the neo-classic conception of an heroic poem,
is limited to such extra-human agents as the personi-
fied Discord of Boileau, and the Envy of Garth, ma-
chines of the same order as the Goddess Dulness, who
was later to preside over Pope's *Dunciad*. By happy
inspiration Pope lighted on a new sort of "machinery," peculiarly suited to his theme, the ele-
mental essences of Paracelsus and the Rosicrucians.
In his dedicatory letter to Mrs. Fermor, Pope explains
the matter thus:

> The machinery, Madam, is a term invented by the
> Critics, to signify that part which the Deities, Angels,
> or Dæmons, are made to act in a Poem. . . . These
> machines I determin'd to raise on a very new and odd
> foundation, the *Rosicrucian* doctrine of Spirits.
>
> The *Rosicrucians* are a people I must bring you
> acquainted with. The best account I know of them is

> in a French Book call'd *Le Comte de Gabalis*, which
> both in its title and size is so like a Novel, that many
> of the Fair Sex have read it for one by mistake. Ac-
> cording to these Gentlemen, the four Elements are
> inhabited by Spirits, which they call *Sylphs*, *Gnomes*,
> *Nymphs*, and *Salamanders*.

Le Comte de Gabalis by the Abbé de Montfaucon de
Villars (1635-1673) was published at Paris in 1670,
and went through many editions. In 1680 had appeared independently two translations of it, by A.
Lovell and by P. Ayres. In 1714, a new translation
was published by Lintot and Curll, the anonymous
translator of which declares in his Preface that it "was
occasion'd by *The Rape of the Lock*."

The *Count of Gabalis* is a very witty and entertaining book, in which by delicate and playful irony the
doctrines of the Rosicrucians are held up to ridicule.
It is made up of five "Discourses," actually dialogues,
in which the Count of Gabalis, a Rosicrucian adept,
instructs the sceptical but open-minded author in the
intricacies of Cabalistic lore:

> The *Salamanders* . . . are compos'd of the most
> subtile Parts of the Sphere of Fire. . . . The *Sylphs*
> are likewise compos'd of the purest Atoms of the Air;
> the *Nymphs*, of the finest Parts of the Water; and the
> *Gnomes*, of the subtilest Parts of the Earth. There was
> a Sort of Sameness between the Ingredients that
> form'd *Adam*, and these so perfect Creatures; because,
> being made up of the very purest Particles of these
> four Elements, he contain'd in himself the Perfections
> of these four Species of People, and was their natural
> Lord and King.[7]

But with the Fall, the harmony was broken. It is for

the adept to recover the sovereignty over these creatures. Only the adept can behold their forms, invisible to other men. They are by nature perishable creatures, who can attain to immortality only by intercourse with a mortal, who to be eligible to mate with them must scrupulously abstain from human love.

Of the Rosicrucian doctrine of spirits Pope has utilized only the names of the four essences, and has chiefly confined himself to the Sylphs and Gnomes; from the same source may come also the detail that Ariel abandons his care of Belinda when he sees "an earthly Lover lurking at her heart." His sylphs owe their name to the Rosicrucians; Pope's conception of them is rather derived from the English fairy-lore of *Midsummer Night's Dream*, the *Tempest*, and Milton's *Comus*, which he has playfully transposed from moonlit glades and enchanted islands to the drawing rooms of Hampton Court.[8] The Ariel of Shakespeare is hardly recognizable in his Augustan namesake; they are as far apart as are Miranda and Belinda. Until Bottom sets them to grosser tasks, it is the duty of Titania's servitors to—

> go seek some dewdrops here
> And hang a pearl in every cowslip's ear.

And Prospero's Ariel sings:

> Where the bee sucks, there suck I:
> In a cowslip's bell I lie;
> There I couch when owls do cry.
> On the bat's back I do fly
> After summer merrily.
> Merrily, merrily shall I live now
> Under the blossom that hangs on the bough.

Pope's Ariel couches, to be sure, on the nosegay in Belinda's breast, but he is equally at home when perched on one of the taking cards in her hand at ombre. When he disposes his airy forces to guard Belinda,

> To fifty chosen *Sylphs*, of special note,
> We trust th' important charge, the Petticoat.

And having taken their stations,

> Some, orb in orb, around the nymph extend,
> Some thrid the mazy ringlets of her hair,
> Some hang upon the pendants of her ear.

Pope's additions to the earlier version include, besides the introduction of the Rosicrucian sylphs, the scene at Belinda's toilet which concludes Canto I, the game at ombre in Canto III, and the whole description of the Cave of Spleen (which is a part of the machinery). The poem which in Lintot's *Miscellany* consisted of 334 lines now numbered 764 lines,[9] and yet no one would from reading the expanded version ever guess that it had not all sprung from a single inspiration. Years afterwards Pope said to Spence (p. 142): "The making that [the machinery], and what was published before, hit so well together, is, I think, one of the greatest proofs of judgment of anything I ever did." The revision is of a curious sort; for the great majority of the lines the text of the 1712 edition is retained unaltered, and the new matter is merely interpolated. Canto III ends with the same paragraph, altered only by two or three words, which had concluded the first canto of the earlier text. Perhaps the only indication that the introduction of the Rosicrucian machinery was an afterthought is the fact, pointed out by Dennis in his very ill-natured and usually wrongheaded *Remarks on the Rape of the Lock* (1728), that the sylphs and gnomes have no effect whatever upon the action of the piece. Dr. Johnson agreed that "it must be allowed to imply some want of art, that their power has not been sufficiently intermingled with the action." Ariel's warning is unheeded; his protection is ineffectual. Everything happens in the expanded poem, precisely as it had happened in the original version. But if the machinery does not affect the action, it contributes enormously to the artistic effect. What had been a witty and graceful *jeu d'esprit* is now the supreme masterpiece of its kind in the whole range of European literature, beside which its models, the *Dispensary* and *Le Lutrin*, sink into insignificance; it is also the supreme masterpiece of Pope's poetic art. Johnson called it "the most attractive of all ludicrous compositions." It is that and much more than that; it is poetry of a very high order, poetry that can "dip in the richest tincture of the skies" images and ideas which would not ordinarily be regarded as the proper matter of poetry.

Suppose one were asked to write today a great poem on a week-end house-party, its heroine an empty-headed débutante, its hero a college undergraduate; its chief episodes a ride in a motor car, the mixing of cocktails, a game of bridge; its story a passing flirtation, in the course of which the undergraduate hero, having accepted a dare, snips a lock from out the débutante heroine's permanent wave. And the poem must not be merely such occasional verse as might become the pages of *Punch* or the *New Yorker*; it must be so great a poem that people will still read it, not only with amusement but with the thrill of poetic delight, two hundred and more years from now, when motor cars and bridge and cocktails and permanent waves may all stand in need of explanatory footnotes. That is what Pope has done. For those readers who in the early spring of 1714 bought from Mr. Bernard Lintot, "at the Cross-Keys in Fleet-street" a copy of the thin octavo volume in its marbled paper wrappers there was none of the romantic glamour which for us pervades the world of Queen Anne's England. For them powdered wigs and knee-buckles and snuff-boxes, the petticoat "stiff with hoops, and arm'd with ribs of whale," were not picturesque fashions of long ago, but familiar matter of today. Mr. Pope's sylphs were fluttering down the columns of society news and the social register.

Hazlitt called the *Rape of the Lock* the "triumph of insignificance." Matters of no inherent consequence at all are handled with triumphant wit and fancy. "The little is made great, and the great little." The sunrise is something essentially great, great with cosmic grandeur. But the sun does not look out through the cloudy curtains of the east to summon men and beasts to the renewal of daily toil.

> *Sol* thro' white curtains shot a tim'rous ray,
> And op'd those eyes that must eclipse the day;
> Now lapdogs give themselves the rousing shake,
> And sleepless lovers, just at twelve, awake.

Belinda at her toilet is given all the ceremonial pomp
of a high priestess at the altar, "each silver Vase in
mystic order laid," the attendant acolyte at her side:

> First, rob'd in white, the nymph intent adores
> With head uncover'd, the cosmetic pow'rs.
> A heav'nly Image in the glass appears,
> To that she bends, to that her eyes she rears;
> Th' inferior Priestess, at her altar's side,
> Trembling, begins the sacred rites of Pride.

Sometimes the effect is gained by a witty coupling of
the great and the little within the limits of a single
sentence:

> Whether the nymph shall break *Diana*'s law,
> Or some frail *China* jar receive a flaw,
> Or stain her honour, or her new Brocade,
> Forget her pray'rs, or miss a masquerade,
> Or lose her heart, or necklace, at a Ball;
> Or whether heav'n has doom'd that *Shock* must fall.

Were one to make a roster of the dogs of English
literature, Belinda's Shock will take high place along
with Mr. Pope's own favourite Bounce. Did not Ariel
constitute himself the particular guard of Shock?

Though a game at cards would seem to most people
matter of commonplace rather than of poetry, there is
buried in the designs of our playing cards a wealth of
poetic fancy, of kings and queens and royal servitors,
which Pope has wizard-like brought back to life in
what is one of the most triumphant passages of his
masterpiece. And he has done it with strict fidelity
to the facts. A little study of the obsolete game of
ombre will enable one to set up the hands of each of
the three players, and play out each of the nine tricks

to the accompaniment of Pope's majestic lines. One
can at least look at the detailed design of the picture
cards which one ordinarily takes for granted. Pope's
deck of cards had full length portraits of its royal personages. Ours have been cut in the middle to make
the cards reversible; but the design has otherwise remained constant. I wonder if Mr. Ely Culbertson
knows that it is the "Club's black Tyrant" who, "of
all monarchs, only grasps the globe."

Sometimes the magic of Pope's poetry is so potent
that he makes us forget that his is a laughing Muse—
in such lines as these, for example:

> But now secure the painted vessel glides,
> The sun-beams trembling on the floating tydes,
> While melting music steals upon the sky,
> And soften'd sounds along the waters die;
> Smooth flow the waves, the zephyrs gently play,
> *Belinda* smil'd, and all the world was gay.

Or again, a few lines farther on, as the guardian sylphs
hover over Belinda's barge:

> Some to the sun their insect-wings unfold,
> Waft on the breeze, or sink in clouds of gold;
> Transparent forms, too fine for mortal sight,
> Their fluid bodies half dissolv'd in light.
> Loose to the wind their airy garments flew,
> Thin glitt'ring textures of the filmy dew;
> Dipt in the richest tinctures of the skies,
> Where light disports in ever-mingling dies,
> While ev'ry beam new transient colours flings,
> Colours that change whene'er they wave their wings.

Pope had not yet learned to write poetry like that in
the days when he was writing the *Pastorals* and
Windsor Forest.

"Triumph of insignificance" though it is, the *Rape of the Lock* is not without some deeper significance. If it makes little things great, is not that what we are continually doing in our social lives? We magnify the importance of dress and correctness of manners; we lose our tempers over trifling annoyances, and make much of trivial slights. Though Lord Petre's offense against Belinda was, after all, something more than trivial annoyance, it was not worth an estrangement between their families. It is on such foibles as these that Pope builds the high comedy of his "heroi-comical" poem. It is comedy rather than satire, I think, though most commentators have used the sterner word in talking about it. Only in the portrait of Sir Plume is there, to my taste, the sting of satire. Pope has not in this poem even so much of satirical rebuke as one finds in the pages of the *Spectator*. Does Pope wish that the hearts of the ladies shall be more than "moving toy-shops"?

But an eighteenth-century poem, even a mock-heroic poem, was expected to teach while it gave delight. To make clearer that his poem recommends the virtues of good humour and good sense, Pope made one final addition to it before he reprinted it in the collected *Works* of 1717. A new character, Clarissa, is introduced "to open," so Pope explains, "more clearly the Moral of the Poem, in a parody of the speech of Sarpedon to Glaucus in Homer":

> Oh! if to dance all night, and dress all day,
> Charm'd the small-pox, or chas'd old age away;

Who would not scorn what huswife's cares produce,
Or who would learn one earthly thing of use?
. . .   .

But since, alas! frail beauty must decay,
Curl'd or uncurl'd, since Locks will turn to grey,
Since painted, or not painted, all shall fade,
And she who scorns a man, must die a maid;
What then remains, but well our pow'r to use,
And keep good humour still whate'er we lose?
And trust me, dear! good humour can prevail,
When airs, and flights, and screams, and scolding fail.
Beauties in vain their pretty eyes may roll;
Charms strike the sight, but merit wins the soul.

Good sense and good humour make up the sum of merit. The first half of the poem draws its central comic idea from the lack of good sense; from the moment when the action reaches its climax as Belinda's lock feels "the conqu'ring force of unresisted steel," the theme becomes the lack of good humour. Trifle though it is, the poem is constructed with the nice craftsmanship of a watchmaker. In the whole of its conduct, in its conception and in its expression, it is the perfect illustration of that balance of wit and judgment which was the goal of neo-classic art. If, as Warton said, Pope has in this poem "displayed more imagination than in all his other works taken together," the imagination is never allowed to outrun the controlling judgment. On any principle of criticism it is a great masterpiece of poetic art, one of the permanent achievements of English poetry.

The poem was instantly recognized for the masterpiece that it is by all competent critics whose judgment was not, like that of poor John Dennis, warped

by personal hostility to the author. Bishop Berkeley
(not yet a bishop) wrote to Pope from Leghorn under
date of May 1, 1714:

> I have accidentally met with your Rape of the Lock
> here, having never seen it before. Style, painting,
> judgment, spirit, I had already admired in other of
> your writings; but in this I am charmed with the
> magic of your invention, with all those images, al-
> lusions, and inexplicable beauties, which you raise so
> surprisingly, and at the same time so naturally out of
> a trifle.

If Pope was pleased by such praise as this from a
"judicious" reader, he and his publisher must also
have been highly gratified by the immediate response
of the general public. It was on March 4, 1714, that
Lintot exposed for sale in a handsome octavo of sixty
pages, with six full-page illustrations designed by
Louis Du Guernier and engraved by C. du Bosc,[10]
"The Rape of the Lock. An Heroi-comical Poem. In
Five Canto's.—Written by Mr. Pope." Eight days
later Pope wrote to his friend Caryll that the book
"has in four days' time sold to the number of three
thousand." Before the end of the year a second and a
third edition were called for, each apparently involv-
ing a complete resetting of the type. A fourth edition
appeared in September, 1715, and a fifth in 1716.

III

In the years immediately preceding 1717 Pope liked
to think of himself as a romantic and very melancholy
person. This, at least, is the recurrent pose of his
letters written in the autumn of 1716 to Lady Mary

Wortley Montagu, as in his thoughts he follows her on her perilous journey to the far-away Levant.

> If I did not take a particular care to disguise it, my letters would be the most melancholy things in the world. . . . The more I examine my own mind, the more romantic I find myself. . . . Let them say I am romantic; so is every one said to be that either admires a fine thing or praises one: it is no wonder such people are thought mad.[11]

Very romantic and most pensively melancholy is the *Elegy to the Memory of an Unfortunate Lady*, first published in the collected *Works* of 1717, where it is called "Verses to the Memory of an Unfortunate Lady."[12] Its opening lines plunge at once into the moonlit gloom of a Gothick romance of terror:

> What beck'ning ghost, along the moonlight shade
> Invites my steps, and points to yonder glade?
> 'Tis she!—but why that bleeding bosom gor'd,
> Why dimly gleams the visionary sword?

Precisely why, the poem never tells us in so many words. The reader must pluck out the heart of the Unfortunate Lady's mystery as best he can. She had had in her make-up something of the romantic rebel, at war with stale convention, which makes of most souls—

> Dull sullen pris'ners in the body's cage:
> Dim lights of life that burn a length of years,
> Useless, unseen, as lamps in sepulchres;

From such a fate as that the sword and bleeding bosom have nobly saved her.

Just when the poem was written, there is no evidence to determine. In the correspondence of Pope

and his friends there is no allusion to it earlier than
the date of its publication. It would seem that Pope's
friend Caryll had not read the poem—though he
thought he remembered that he had once heard a
similar story—until he met it on the printed page; for
in a letter of July 16, 1717, he wrote to Pope:

> Your works are my daily lecture, and with what
> satisfaction I need not repeat to you. But pray, in
> your next, tell me who was the unfortunate lady you
> address a copy of verses to. I think you once gave me
> her history, but it is now quite out of my head.

Had Caryll read so striking a poem and heard from
the poet the lady's history, it is most unlikely that it
could have gone out of his head. Pope in his reply to
this letter had ignored Caryll's question, and Caryll
asks it again in his next letter of August 18. So far as
the correspondence preserved to us indicates, Caryll's
curiosity was never satisfied. The reason for Pope's
failure to answer the question was pretty certainly
that the Unfortunate Lady is completely the creation
of his romantic imagination.

Pope's biographers for a hundred years after his
death tried their best to find an original. The worth-
less *Memoirs of the Life and Writings of Alexander
Pope, Esq.*, which purports to have been written by
one William Ayre, and which was hastily published
in the year succeeding the poet's death, tells an
elaborate story that is actually only an embellishment of the data that can be derived from the poem
itself.[13] And succeeding biographers down to Bowles
have recorded whatever hearsay answer may have

come their way. It is not strange that people should
have been curious; for the closing lines of the poem
suggest, and are certainly intended to suggest, that the
nameless lady was someone dearly loved by the poet:

> Ev'n he, whose soul now melts in mournful lays,
> Shall shortly want the gen'rous tear he pays;
> Then from his closing eyes thy form shall part,
> And the last pang shall tear thee from his heart,
> Life's idle business at one gasp be o'er,
> The Muse forgot, and thou belov'd no more!

The only answer Pope ever gave to the natural
query, "Who is it?", is given in a footnote with his
initial in Warburton's edition of 1751:

> See the Duke of Buckingham's verses to a Lady
> designing to retire into a Monastery compared with
> Mr. Pope's Letters to Several Ladies, p. 206, quarto
> edition. She seems to be the same person whose un-
> fortunate death is the subject of this poem.

In the Works of John Sheffield, Duke of Buckingham
(1648-1721), which Pope himself edited in 1723, one
finds (Vol. I, pp. 76-9) a poem entitled "To a Lady
retiring into a Monastery." Between this poem and
Pope's *Elegy* it is impossible to discover any resemblance whatsoever. Buckingham's poem implies that
the lady addressed is his mistress, and in 1716 or 1717
his grace would have been a very elderly lover. Pope's
reference to his own correspondence is equally un-
illuminating. Page 206 yields no results at all; but on
page 86 one picks up a clue that seems to lead one to a
certain Mrs. Weston, a lady unhappily married, whose
cause Pope and Caryll had chivalrously espoused in
the year 1712. Save that she had a guardian whom

Pope thought remiss in his care of her, there is no similarity whatever between the fortunes of Mrs. Weston, who died quite normally in 1724, and those of the Unfortunate Lady of the *Elegy*.[14]

It is quite clear that the lady of "beauty, titles, wealth, and fame," who, aspiring "above the vulgar flight of low desire" had "loved too well," and who, deserted by her "false guardian," her uncle, had in a foreign land gored her bosom with a sword, and had been buried in unhallowed ground, her grave unadorned save by "rising flowers," is completely the creation of Pope's romantic imagination. So far as sober fact is concerned, she was never more substantial than the "beck'ning ghost" of the poem, and the sword which gored her bosom was from the beginning but "visionary." She is in intensity of passion, and in superiority to the conventions, own sister to Pope's Eloisa (who also had a cruel guardian-uncle) and may well owe her creation to the same poetic impulse. But Pope, who always knew what would best hold his reader, thought it better to hint at a real Unfortunate whose form only death could sever from the poet's melting soul. And then the Rules demanded that the elegiac poet must himself know the pangs of unhappy love. Had not Boileau in that translation by Soames which Pope had read and annotated so decreed?

> The *Elegy*, that loves a mournful stile,
> With unbound hair weeps at a Funeral Pile,
> . . . .
> But well these Raptures if you'l make us see,
> You must know Love, as well as Poetry.

Otherwise his "feign'd Transports appear but flat and vain." And so Pope, while the poem was recent, gave no answer to the inquiry of his friends, and then in his later years wrote the misleading, but cautiously vague, annotation which Warburton has printed. Pope would have been delighted could he have read Warton's critique of his only elegy:

> If this Elegy be so excellent, it may be ascribed to this cause; that the occasion of it was real; for it is certainly an indisputable maxim, "That nature is more powerful than fancy; that we can always feel more than we can imagine; and that the most artful fiction must give way to truth."[15]

I think that most modern readers will find it less "tender and pathetic" than did Warton; they may even find much of it theatrical rather than genuinely tragic—particularly the lines that denounce "sudden vengeance" on the false guardian, and threaten his gates with "frequent herses." Its literary virtues spring not from Pope's heart, but from his exquisite mastery of the art of poetic expression; or perhaps it would be nearer the truth to say that the poet's heart was deeply enlisted in his passionate devotion to the Muse. For the poem is written with poetic fire, which blazes with indignation, or glows in such an exquisite lyricism as the lines which deck the Unfortunate Lady's nameless grave:

> What tho' no sacred earth allow thee room,
> Nor hallow'd dirge be mutter'd o'er thy tomb?
> Yet shall thy grave with rising flow'rs be drest,
> And the green turf lie lightly on thy breast:

There shall the morn her earliest tears bestow,
There the first roses of the year shall blow;
While Angels with their silver wings o'ershade
The ground, now sacred by thy reliques made.

Pope's Elegy is most musical as well as most melancholy. I think that most readers will dissent from Dr. Johnson's very Johnsonian verdict that "Poetry has not often been worse employed than in dignifying the amorous fury of a raving girl."

If Pope wished the world to think that the *Verses to the Memory of an Unfortunate Lady* came from a heart which knew the pangs of love, he is similarly concerned to suggest that he was "joined in sad similitude of griefs" to the unfortunate Eloisa. Of her griefs also it is true that "he best can paint 'em, who shall feel 'em most." At the time he was writing these poems, he was doing his best to persuade not only others but himself that he was a woe-begone lover. To Lady Mary Wortley Montagu, far away in Turkey, who had not yet been metamorphosed into slovenly "Sappho," he addressed between the summer of 1716 and the autumn of 1718 most lover-like epistles. In June of 1717 he sent her the third volume of Homer and a copy of the newly published *Works*. In the letter which accompanied them he wrote:

> You have all I am worth, that is, my works: there are few things in them but what you have already seen, except the Epistle of Eloisa to Abelard, in which you will find one passage [surely the concluding lines], that I cannot tell whether to wish you should understand, or not.

About a year earlier he had written to another lady, Mrs. Martha Blount, as follows:

> The Epistle of Eloisa grows warm, and begins to have some breathings of the heart in it, which may make posterity think I was in love. I can scarce find in my heart to leave out the conclusion I once intended for it.[16]

Had Pope already shown his conclusion to Martha Blount and told her that it was directed towards her? There is more than a little pathos in the poor cripple's attempts to pretend that he is in love at the same time that his poetry is turning on themes of love's frustration. For *Eloisa* as well as for the *Unfortunate Lady*, the poet should, according to the Rules, be in love; for though it is in form an epistle, its temper is no less elegaic.[17]

IV

It was not until the reign of Louis XIV that Eloisa assumed, even in her own land of France, the place which has been hers ever since as one of the great names in the kalendar of romantic love.[18] In 1687, the year before Pope's birth and just thirty years before the publication of his *Eloisa*, that rather disreputable, but very witty, gentleman, Roger de Rabutin, Comte de Bussy, author of the *Histoires Amoureuses des Gaules*, translated, or freely paraphrased, into French prose the first of Eloisa's letters to Abelard, Abelard's reply, and Eloisa's response to Abelard—Letters II, III, and IV of the Latin text. In 1695 Bussy's translation, revised by Remond des Cours, and extended by an unidentified continuator to include the *Historia*

Calamitatum (Letter I, written by Abelard to his friend Philinthus) and two letters numbered V and VI which have no Latin original and are completely spurious, was published at The Hague. The "translations" are preceded by an *Histoire des Amours et Infortunes d'Abélard et d'Eloise* by N. F. Dubois.[19] This duodecimo volume, republished in 1697, 1700, 1703, 1705, 1709, and 1711, gave wide popularity to a very seriously distorted Eloisa and Abelard. The Letters, when not utterly spurious, are at best a free paraphrase. They are a free paraphrase not only in their substance, with omissions, additions, and rearrangements, but even more in tone and temper. The broken and embittered Abelard of the Latin letters is a rather forbidding figure; in Eloisa the ardours of a passionate love are balanced by a fine austerity of spirit; despite the embellishments of medieval rhetoric, and the learned citation of authorities, she writes with a compelling directness of utterance which wins not only sympathy but full respect. In the pages of the Bussy-Rabutin translation both the passion and the rhetoric are of the school of Mlle. de Scudéry.

It was the Eloisa of Bussy-Rabutin and his continuators, and not of the original Letters, that from Pope to Rousseau was to rule the imagination of the eighteenth century.

All that Pope knew of Abelard and Eloisa he derived from a rather close translation into English of the French of Bussy-Rabutin published in 1714 by his friend John Hughes. There is nothing to suggest that he had ever seen Hughes's French original, and it seems quite certain that he made no use of the Latin originals—which, in their austerity, would have seemed to him rather disappointing. To Hughes, Pope owes the substance (or one might better say the raw material) of more than half of his lines. Sometimes it is a suggestion which Pope develops, sometimes the very language of Hughes is retained. But Pope has not made a poetical paraphrase of one of the letters; he has instead made a mosaic of matters picked here and there from the whole collection—even words which were Abelard's are in Pope spoken by Eloisa.

If the matter of Pope's poem came, by way of Hughes, from the French of Bussy-Rabutin and his continuators, the form is that of Ovid's *Heroides*, in which the mythical ladies of heroic antiquity address to their absent and usually faithless lovers, in highly wrought elegiac verse, rhetorical complaints that also retell a familiar story. Though the heroines are all from the world of long ago, Ovid makes no attempt to re-create a more primitive society; his ladies, though involved in romantic circumstance, think and speak and feel like completely sophisticated ladies of Augustan Rome. They are all unfortunate ladies, but rarely do they attain to authentic tragedy. Instead of tragedy we have sometimes pathos, sometimes the merely sentimental and picturesque, sometimes only an ingenious playing with words. Virgil's Dido is a very womanly figure, but she is also an heroic and essentially tragic figure; Ovid's Dido is not so much womanly as very feminine.

From the time of Chaucer the *Heroides* had been familiar to English readers. In 1567 George Turberville translated them, some in blank verse, some in alternating sevens and sixes, into vigorous Elizabethan English. In 1637 they were very clumsily rendered by Wye Saltonstall in five-stress couplets; and, more competently, in 1639 by John Sherburne, Gent. In 1680, Tonson brought out "Ovid's Epistles, Translated by Several Hands," in which the Preface and three of the epistles were done by Dryden. It was for the eighth edition of this translation (1712) that Pope contributed his translation of the epistle of Sappho to Phaon.

The *Heroides* were not only translated but imitated. In 1619 was published Michael Drayton's *England's Heroicall Epistles*. The imagined writers of these epistles are the ladies and gentlemen of English history. There are letters to and from Fair Rosamond and Henry II, Matilda and King John, Queen Isabel and Mortimer, Jane Shore and Edward IV. In 1703 appeared "*Amores Britannici*. Epistles Historical and Gallant, In English Heroic Verse From several of the most Illustrious Personages of their Times. In Imitation of the *Heroidum Epistolae* of Ovid." The "Epistle Dedicatory" is signed T. Oldmixon. It is, as Oldmixon frankly states, a reversification of Drayton; but Oldmixon has added exchanges of letters between Queen Elizabeth and the Earl of Essex, Mary Queen of the Scots and the Duke of Norfolk, and the Countess of

Carlisle and Mr. Waller. Oldmixon tells us what such poems as these should be:

> If Passion and Nature are the distinguishing character of such Epistles, if the Sentiments shou'd be gallant and tender, the Language easie and musical, and nothing to appear forc'd and affected; perhaps the Criticks will not dislike this performance. . . .

The performance is, however, a very dull one. The reader will be much better advised to read Drayton rather than his modernizer. It seems not unlikely, however, that despite his contempt for "unlucky Oldmixon," Pope may have caught from him the idea that an epistle in the manner of Ovid might be made from the letters of Eloisa and Abelard.[20]

A suggestion so derived might have been reinforced by the great popularity of the *Letters of a Portuguese Nun*. Marianna Alcoforado (1640-1721) had been abandoned by her lover, an officer of the French army. To him she wrote from her nunnery a series of reproachful love-letters.[21] Published at Paris in 1669, they became at once one of the sensations of the day. They were translated into English by Sir Roger L'Estrange in 1678.[22] Only a few years before the composition of Pope's *Eloisa* they had twice been versified in English. The prose letters, though an interesting human document, are the record of a commonplace *amour*, and have none of the elevation of spirit nor the intellectual substance of the letters which the French nun, Eloisa, wrote to her sometime lover.

The verse-epistle of unhappy love was, then, a form very much in vogue in the early decades of the eighteenth century; and the letters of Eloisa and Abelard, reshaped into the temper of late seventeenth-century France, provided ideal material to pour into this form. If read against the background of its provenance, Pope's *Eloisa* will be more adequately appraised by the modern reader. He will at least understand certain qualities in it which may offend his taste, and he will at the same time realize how immeasurably it surpasses all its prototypes, not excepting the *Heroic Epistles* of Ovid. It is, for example, quite beside the point to object that Pope has given us no re-creation of life in the twelfth century. Pope's generation had not yet caught our more modern zeal for re-creating the past; was it not the ideal of poetry that it should achieve a universal which is timeless? The heroines of Ovid are the poet's contemporary countrywomen, with no flavour of ancient Carthage or the wind-swept plains of Troy clinging to their garments. Even had Pope wished to give us a twelfth-century Eloisa, how could he have done so? The authentic medievalism of the original Latin letters had been transformed into something very different by the author of the *Histoires Amoureuses des Gaules*. Similarly, one will understand that, in the tradition to which it belongs, Pope's *Eloisa* could hardly avoid being somewhat over-ornate and somewhat too obviously rhetorical. It is idle to object that there is in its composition more of artifice than nature, that its pathos is a studied pathos.

If Pope has surpassed in poetic power all his models, it is in part because of his greater artistry, in part because his theme is superior in imaginative values and potential significance. Even the sentimentalizing which Eloisa underwent at the hands of her seventeenth-century French remodellers has not obliterated the fact that she is not only a great lover, but an abiding symbol. In his Argument to the poem Pope says that the Letters give "a lively picture of the struggles of grace and nature, virtue and passion." Such a struggle is impossible for Ovid's heroines. Pagan antiquity could understand the conflict of virtue and passion—though to so polished, yet undisciplined, a son of this world as Publius Ovidius Naso it would doubtless have savoured of "rusticity," which was his term for what his modern equivalents are pleased to dismiss as "bourgeois morality." The conflict of "grace and nature" is on a level higher than that of even the greatest of the pagans. For Eloisa there is no problem of conduct; her way of life, so far as the *vita activa* is concerned, is irrevocably settled and rigorously ordered. It is within the realm of the *vita contemplativa* that the conflict rages—"rebel nature holds out half" the heart which should entirely "quit Abelard for God."

This conflict Pope has seized on as the mainspring of his poem. Somewhat too insistently, perhaps, he has pushed the antithesis of the love spiritual and the love carnal, so that Eloisa is rather the exemplification of a theme than an imaginatively realized person. Pope has not identified himself with his personage as Shakespeare and Chaucer and Browning

seem to do, but has rather worked her up from without. But the antithesis has clothed itself in images of
high and great beauty and in exquisitely musical
numbers in such lines as these:

> I waste the Matin lamp in sighs for thee,
> Thy image steals between my God and me,
> Thy voice I seem in ev'ry hymn to hear,
> With ev'ry bead I drop too soft a tear.
> When from the Censer clouds of fragrance roll,
> And swelling organs lift the rising soul;
> One thought of thee puts all the pomp to flight,
> Priests, Tapers, Temples, swim before my sight;
> In seas of flame my plunging soul is drown'd,
> While Altars blaze, and Angels tremble round. (267-76)

This is poetry of a high order; but it is, I think, lyric
poetry—the sort of lyric that one meets in an exalted
ode—rather than essentially dramatic. And it is Pope
rather than Eloisa who is singing for us. He has built
the passage up from a single sentence in his original.
In the pages of Hughes he had read: "Even into holy
places before the altar, I carry with me the memory
of our guilty loves." All the rest is the poet's fine invention. It is not from Hughes, but from memories of
Horace, of Crashaw, of Milton, and of Dryden (and
perhaps also of the Song of Songs) that Pope has
educed what is probably the most beautiful lyric
flight in the whole poem, the lines (207-22) which
begin—

> How happy is the blameless vestal's lot.

There is hardly anything in the letters as Pope
read them (or in the original Latin, for that matter) of

the romantic setting which Pope has provided for his
piece, and which he has skillfully introduced into the
texture of the epistolary monologue. The actual Con-
vent of the Paraclete, near Nogent-sur-Seine (of
which only a few vestiges now remain), was located in
a quite unromantic level country; and, since it had
been established by Abelard for Eloisa, it must in her
day have been unromantically new and spick-and-
span. Unmindful of all this, Pope has given to it and
its surroundings the romantic wildness of the Grande
Chartreuse:

> Relentless walls! whose darksom round contains
> Repentant sighs, and voluntary pains:
> Ye rugged rocks! which holy knees have worn;
> Ye grots and caverns shagg'd with horrid thorn!   (17-20)
> . . .   .
> The darksom pines that o'er yon' rocks reclin'd
> Wave high, and murmur to the hollow wind;
> The wandering streams that shine between the hills,
> The grots that eccho to the tinkling rills,   (155-8)
> . . .   .
> But o'er the twilight groves, and dusky caves,
> Long-sounding isles, and intermingled graves,
> Black Melancholy sits, and round her throws
> A death-like silence, and a dread repose!
> Her gloomy presence saddens all the scene,
> Shades ev'ry flow'r, and darkens ev'ry green,
> Deepens the murmur of the falling floods,
> And breathes a browner horror on the woods. (163-70)

It is against this Gainsborough-like gloom of background that Eloisa utters her elegiac complaint for
the love that can never be recovered, and tears her
soul in the conflict between Abelard and God.

V

The folded frontispiece of the 1717 volume is a line
engraving by George Vertue after a portrait by Sir
Godfrey Kneller.[23] Within a foliated oval frame rest-
ing on a stone wall-bracket is the half-length portrait of the young poet, his body turned to the
reader's left, his head turned partly back to the right.
His right hand, with exceptionally long fingers, in the
manner of Van Dyke, rests lightly against his body.
He is wearing an elaborately curled full-bottomed
wig; his shirt is open at the throat. It is the portrait
of a gallant young gentleman in his middle twenties,
slender, erect, with no suggestion of deformity. The
features are delicately modelled—high forehead,
arched eyebrows which almost meet, long straight
nose, sensitive but strong mouth, firmly modelled
lips that suggest a certain fastidious disdain. It is a
completely romantic figure, every inch a poet. It is
this portrait of Pope, rather than the quizzical portrait by Richardson in the National Portrait Gallery
or the Roubillac bust, that would have lingered in
men's memories, and coloured their reading of the
man and the poet, had Pope died ten years before the
Dunciad.

Though his premature death would have deprived
us of some of his most brilliant literary achievements,
it would, I think, have made more secure for the
nineteenth century his position as a great poet. The
bitter animosities which came to a head a decade
later with the campaign against the Dunces, and
which have continued to plague his memory with

many an unfounded slander, were in 1718 limited to a
few not very important enmities. The unworthy
stratagems and indirections of his later years, particularly those that have to do with the translation
of the *Odyssey* and the publication of his correspondence, had not yet put their mark on his personal
character. It is Pope the satirist to whom hostile
critics have given the sobriquet of the "wasp of
Twickenham," a sobriquet which wilfully ignores his
generosity to younger poets and the sweet kindliness
of nature which he constantly revealed to his friends.
There can be no doubt that to many readers of poetry
throughout the nineteenth century, Pope the man
was an entirely unsympathetic figure; and for nearly
every one in that century, at any rate, it was difficult
to dissociate a work of art from the personal character of the artist. All that personal prejudice would
have been averted if Pope had died in 1718; instead
we should have had another sentimentalized figure of
the young poet cut off in the first flower of his genius
—and a genius which was apparently to develop into
the great precursor of the romantic movement!

But Pope chose to live a while longer. The decade
from 1718 to 1728 was occupied with Homeric translation and the slipshod editing of Shakespeare; and
then stepped forth the satirist and poetic moralist,
whose literary virtues, however great, were not of the
romantic order.

V

HOMER SPEAKS GOOD ENGLISH

LOVERS of good poetry who in the summer of
1717 read in Lintot's handsome folio volume the
collected *Works* of Mr. Pope, and delightedly hailed
him as a genius of the first order, may well have expected that the immediately ensuing years would see
new and even greater triumphs of his Muse. But
Pope's Muse already had her hands full with the work
of finding apt words and numbers for the rendering of
Homer. So completely were his energies given to the
work of translation and annotation—and later to the
editing of Shakespeare—that the world was to see no
original poem of any consequence until the *Dunciad*
of 1728. It must not be forgotten that Pope's *Iliad*—
not to mention his share in the *Odyssey*—involved the
composition of nearly 19,000 well-turned lines of
verse, a number of lines greater than that of all his
other poetry put together.

Homer had been from Pope's very early years a
favourite poet. In a letter written in June, 1715, Pope
said to Broome: "he was the first author that made
me catch the itch of poetry, when I read him in my
childhood." And Spence (p. 276) under the years
1742-43 has this entry:

> Ogilby's translation of Homer was one of the first
> large poems that ever Mr. Pope read; and he still
> spoke of the pleasure it then gave him, with a sort of
> rapture, only in reflecting on it.—"It was that great

edition with pictures, I was then about eight years old."

Ogilby's *Iliad*, as published in 1660, was in very truth a "great edition," a sumptuous large-paper folio[1] with fifty or more full-page illustrations. The engravings, though many of them will now make the judicious smile, could well have captivated the imagination of a little boy, still too young to recognize how dull and wooden was Ogilby's rendering of Homer's verse.

Before he was twenty, Pope had tried his own hand at the translation of Homer with a rendering of the episode of Sarpedon from the twelfth and sixteenth books of the *Iliad*, published along with the *Pastorals* in Tonson's *Miscellany* of 1709. Pope had submitted this translation to Sir William Trumbull, who in a letter dated April 9, 1708, wrote thus:

> I entirely approve of your translation of those pieces of Homer, both as to the versification and the true sense that shines through the whole: nay, I am confirmed in my former application to you, and give me leave to renew it upon this occasion, that you would proceed in translating that incomparable poet, to make him speak good English, to dress his admirable characters in your proper, significant, and expressive conceptions, and to make his works as useful and instructive to this degenerate age, as he was to our friend Horace, when he read him at Præneste.[2]

Pope listened to this advice, reinforced, he tells us, by that of Addison, and five years later, in October, 1713, he issued "Proposals for a Translation of Homer's Iliad, with critical and explanatory Notes, by Mr. Pope. To be printed in six Volumes, on the finest Paper. . . ."[3] The price to subscribers was to be a guinea a volume. Pope's friends subscribed themselves and busily solicited the subscriptions of others. Swift, who had on March 9, 1713, praised *Windsor Forest* in his *Journal to Stella*, was particularly energetic in his solicitations. He is reported to have said that "the author shall not begin to print till I have a thousand guineas for him."[4] When, in 1714, Steele published in two volumes the collected edition of the *Guardian*, after enumerating in his prefatory address to the reader Pope's contributions to the periodical, he continued thus:

> Now I mention this Gentleman, I take this opportunity, out of the Affection I have for his Person, and Respect to his Merit, to let the world know, that He is now Translating *Homer's Iliad* by Subscription. He has given good Proof of his Ability for the Work, and the Men of greatest Wit and Learning of this Nation, of all Parties, are, according to their different Abilities, zealous Encouragers, or Sollicitors for the Work.

The list of subscribers prefixed to the first volume, when it appeared on June 6, 1715, showed that these "Encouragers or Sollicitors" had been highly successful. It is a very distinguished list of notables. There is a grand array of dukes and marquises and belted earls, several of whom subscribed for as many as ten sets. Of greater interest to the modern reader are such names as Addison, Arbuthnot, Berkeley, Bolingbroke, Cibber, Congreve, Garth, Gay, Parnell, Prior, Rowe, Steele, Swift, Young, Sir Isaac Newton, and Sir Christopher Wren. There were in all 574 subscribers, who put themselves down for a total of 654 sets. If there were no defaulters, Pope could count on the handsome sum of 3,924 guineas—nearly four times the amount which Swift had set as his goal. Since Bernard Lintot, the publisher, agreed to provide the subscribers' copies without cost to the author, and in addition paid Pope a total of £1,275 for the copyright,[5] Pope's gross receipts amounted to more than £5,000. From the *Odyssey* Pope received three or four thousand more. So that, all told, Homer made for his translator a clear profit of hardly less than £8,000—a very handsome sum indeed, when one remembers that of most of the commodities which make life pleasant a pound sterling of George I purchased many times more than a pound of George VI.[6]

If it was a very profitable undertaking, it was also very laborious—laborious by virtue of its magnitude alone, apart from considerations of scholarship and literary craft. Pope's knowledge of the Greek language was, as his enemies vociferously pointed out, far from that of the exact scholar; but for the sort of task which he set himself exact scholarship was not a matter of primary importance. There were earlier translations, in Latin, French, and English, which he could diligently compare. He could enlist the services of Edward Broome, a fully competent Grecian, to translate and digest for his use the Greek commentary on Homer by the twelfth-century Byzantine scholar Eustathius, and of Thomas Parnell, who wrote the long introductory "Essay on the Life, Writings, and Learning of Homer," which fills pages 1-63 of Volume I.[7]

Broome and Parnell could help him to assemble the
materials for his commentary, and could unravel for
him difficult passages of the original; but it was Pope
himself who must make Homer "speak good English"
through many weary thousands of lines. As he came
fully to realize how large a task he had undertaken, he
was filled with dismay. Five or six years before his
death he confessed to Spence (p. 218) how great the
dismay had been:

> What terrible moments does one feel, after one has
> engaged for a large work!—In the beginning of my
> translating the Iliad, I wished any body would hang
> me, a hundred times.—It sat so heavily on my mind
> at first, that I often used to dream of it, and do some-
> times still.—When I fell into the method of translat-
> ing thirty or forty verses before I got up, and piddled
> with it the rest of the morning, it went on easy
> enough; and when I was thoroughly got into the way
> of it, I did the rest with pleasure.

In a letter dated July 28, 1714—just four days before
the death of Queen Anne—addressed to his painter
friend, Charles Jervas, Pope playfully describes his
complete absorption in his task:

> What can you expect from a man who has not
> talked these five days? Who is withdrawing his
> thoughts, as far as he can, from all the present world,
> its customs and its manners, to be fully possessed and
> absorbed in the past? When people talk of going to
> church, I think of sacrifices and libations; when I see
> the parson, I address him as Chryses, priest of Apollo;
> and instead of the Lord's Prayer, I begin,
>
> God of the silver bow, &c.

> While you in the world are concerned about the
> protestant succession, I consider only how Menelaus
> may recover Helen, and the Trojan war be put to a
> speedy conclusion. I never inquire if the queen be
> well or not, but heartily wish to be at Hector's
> funeral.

It was the same playful conceit which John Gay was
to elaborate in 1720, when at last, with Hector's
funeral achieved, the long task had been brought to
completion, in *Mr. Pope's Welcome from Greece*, "A
Copy of Verses written by Mr. Gay, upon Mr. Pope's
having finished his Translation of Homer's Iliad":

> Hail to the Bard whom long as lost we mourn'd,
> Safe from the Fights of Ten years War return'd.[8]

If Pope thus in imagination naturalized himself as a
citizen of ancient Greece, it was with the conscious
purpose of capturing the very essence of Homer's
spirit, so that he might bring him captive back to
Augustan England. The authentic Homer must be
made to "speak good English." In his Preface, Pope
discusses at some length the proper method of translation. One should find the happy mean between the
too literal and the too free. The substance of the poem,
its Fable, Manners, and Sentiments, and "every
particular *Image*, *Description*, and *Simile*" must be
faithfully preserved, unprejudiced by "wilful Omissions or Contractions." "It is the first grand Duty of
an Interpreter to give his Author entire and un-
maim'd; and for the rest, the *Diction* and *Versification* only are his proper Province; since these must be
his own." But, as Pope was clearly aware, diction and

versification are not external trappings, but integral
elements of the poetic whole. If they are wrong, all
will be wrong.

> It should then be consider'd what Methods may
> afford some Equivalent in our Language for the
> Graces of these in the *Greek*. It is certain no literal
> Translation can be just to an excellent Original in a
> superior Language: but it is a great mistake to im-
> agine (as many have done) that a rash Paraphrase
> can make amends for this general Defect; which is no
> less in danger to lose the Spirit of an Ancient, by de-
> viating into the modern Manners of Expression. . . .
> I know no Liberties one ought to take, but those
> which are necessary for transfusing the Spirit of the
> Original, and supporting the Poetical Style of the
> Translation: and I will venture to say, there have not
> been more Men misled in former times by a servile
> dull Adherence to the Letter, than have been deluded
> in ours by a chimerical insolent Hope of raising and
> improving their Author. (Fol. E 2, verso)

Pope is alluding in these sentences to what had been
in seventeenth-century France a much-disputed topic
of criticism. There were those who argued for the
virtue of strict fidelity. The opposing view was that
the translator should rather make his author speak as
he might have spoken had he been, not an ancient
Greek or Roman, but a seventeenth-century French-
man or Englishman. Sir John Denham takes the
liberal side in his commendatory verses prefixed to
Sir Richard Fanshawe's translation of Guarini's
Pastor Fido (1647):

> That servile path thou nobly dost decline,
> Of tracing word by word and line by line.

A new and nobler way thou dost pursue,
To make Translations and Translators too;
They but preserve the Ashes, Thou the Flame,
True to his sense, but truer to his fame.[9]

Pope has chosen a middle way between the license of free paraphrase and the "servile path" of following the dead letter. With his theory of poetical translation I imagine that few critics would wish to quarrel; the objection will rather be that the "Spirit of the Original" has been transmuted rather than "transfused." Pope has, to be sure, been in certain particulars faithful to the Greek. He has, for example, kept the bulk of the translation very close to that of the original. On the average five lines of the Greek are represented by six lines of the English; but this percentage of increment is exactly balanced by the fact that the Greek line is hexameter and the English line pentameter.[10]

The careful scrutiny of critics, many of them hostile critics, has convicted Pope of very few downright errors in his understanding of his original. But, in a translation so conceived and executed as Pope's, conviction of such error is not easy. What Pope has given us is seldom close translation. Nor is it, in the ordinary meaning of the word, paraphrase; it is rather a poetical re-creation. Homer's images have been poetically reimagined, his ideas reconceived. Details which in Homer are implicit but not immediately expressed are by Pope explicitly recorded. What I mean can best be made clear by illustration, and such illustration may be found on almost any page of

Pope's Homer. At the beginning of Book III the two opposing armies advance against one another. As the Greeks cross the plain, their tramping feet stir up a great cloud of dust. I shall give the passage first in a closely literal translation:

> As when on the crests of a mountain Notus has poured out mist, to shepherds not at all pleasing, but for a thief better than night, and a man sees before him only so far as he can throw a stone; so under their feet as they went the eddying dust arose; and very swiftly they crossed over the plain. (III, 10-14)

The five lines of the Greek have become in the English five couplets, and the expansion results from a more detailed explicitness of statement. In the passage, as Pope has re-created it, I have called attention by italics to details which are Pope's rather than Homer's:

> Swift march the Greeks: the rapid Dust around
> *Dark'ning* arises from the *labour'd* Ground.
> Thus *from his flaggy Wings* when Notus sheds
> A *Night of* Vapors round the Mountain-Heads,
> *Swift-gliding Mists the dusky Fields invade,*
> To Thieves more grateful than the Midnight *Shade*;
> While scarce the Swains their feeding Flocks survey,
> *Lost and confus'd amidst the thicken'd Day*:
> So *wrapt in gath'ring Dust*, the Grecian Train
> *A moving Cloud*, swept on, and hid the Plain.   (III, 13-22)

In Homer the simile of swirling mountain mist precedes the dust-storm which it illustrates; in Pope's re-creation we have first the marching Greeks and the dust, then the simile of mist, and at the end a studied confusion of dust and marching Greeks. Homer is content merely to suggest what the mist does to the shepherds. Pope has elaborated the suggestion and substituted his elaboration for Homer's statement that one can see only a stone's throw—a statement which to Pope may have seemed lacking in poetical elevation. The "flaggy wings" of the south wind are reminiscent of Spenser's dragon, before whose flight even the clouds fled for terror.[11]

The lines which immediately follow those just quoted show another aspect of Pope's imaginative reworking. In his "Observation" on Verse 26 of the Third Book, Pope remarks: "The Picture here given of *Paris's* Air and Dress, is exactly correspondent to his Character; you see him endeavouring to mix the fine Gentleman with the Warriour." And so in his translation Pope has added to Homer's simple "picture" details of his own imagining, which give full emphasis to this idea of the "fine Gentleman" mixed with the warrior. Again, I shall give first a closely literal translation of the Greek:

> So when [the two armies] were now advanced near to one another, godlike Paris stood forth as champion for the Trojans, having on his shoulders a panther-skin and curved bow and sword; and, shaking two bronze-headed spears, he challenged all of the best of the Greeks to fight against him in dreadful combat. (III, 15-20)

As before, I have printed in italics the words and phrases which are the modern poet's imaginative elaborations:

> Now Front to Front the *hostile* Armies stand,
> *Eager of Fight, and only wait Command*:

When, to the Van, *before the Sons of Fame*
Whom Troy *sent forth*, the *beauteous* Paris came:
In Form a God! the Panther's *speckled* Hyde
Flow'd o'er his Armour with an easy Pride,
His bended Bow a-cross his Shoulders flung,
His Sword *beside him negligently hung*,
Two pointed Spears he shook *with gallant Grace*,
And dar'd the Bravest of the Grecian Race.   (III, 23-32)

Far as this is from Homer, it is at least consistently imagined; but I am afraid that Pope had forgotten what he had said in his Preface of translators who indulge "a chimerical insolent Hope of raising and improving their Author." It would be hard to find a single paragraph in which Pope has not to some extent "raised and improved."

It is where Homer is in his more exalted moods—and so less in need of "raising and improving"—that Pope is most adequate in his rendering. "That which in my Opinion ought to be the Endeavour of any one who translates *Homer*, is above all things to keep alive that Spirit and Fire which makes his chief Character," Pope declares in his Preface. It is where Homer's fire burns most ardently that his translator has best succeeded in keeping the flame alive. As a specimen of Pope at his best one may take such a passage as the following, which in the prose translation of Lang, Leaf, and Myers runs thus:

> He spake and leapt in his armour from the chariot to earth, and terribly rang the bronze upon the chieftain's breast as he moved; thereat might fear have come even upon one stout-hearted. As when on the echoing beach the sea-wave lifteth up itself in close

array before the driving of the west wind; out on the
deep doth it first raise its head, and then breaketh
upon the land and belloweth aloud and goeth with
arching crest about the promontories, and speweth
the foaming brine afar; even so in close array moved
the battalions of the Danaans without pause to
battle. Each captain gave his men the word, and the
rest went silently.   (IV, 419-29)

With some addition of poetical rhetoric, though not
more, I think, than a translator may properly be
allowed, this passage becomes in Pope:

He spoke, and ardent on the trembling Ground
Sprung from his Car; his ringing Arms resound.
Dire was the Clang, and dreadful from afar,
Of arm'd *Tydides* rushing to the War.
As when the Winds, ascending by degrees,
First move the whitening Surface of the Seas,
The Billows float in order to the Shore,
The Wave behind rolls on the Wave before;
Till, with the growing Storm, the Deeps arise,
Foam o'er the Rocks, and thunder to the Skies.
So to the Fight the thick *Battalions* throng,
Shields urg'd on Shields, and Men drove Men along.
Sedate and silent move the num'rous Bands;
No Sound, no Whisper, but their Chief's Commands.
(IV, 474-87)

The poetic substance of these lines is in all essentials
that of Homer; the diction and versification, which
are Pope's, transfuse not inadequately the spirit and
energy and fire of the original—more adequately, I
think, than the mannerized, Biblical prose of Messrs.
Lang, Leaf, and Myers. Such passages as this—and
they are by no means infrequent—make Pope's
rendering a brilliant achievement. One can see that

for the readers of his own generation, at least, here was authentic poetry.

Pope is less happy when Homer is in his simpler manner, where poetic elevation is achieved by an exquisite rightness of image and a relatively unadorned directness of statement. Probably the most famous passage of the *Iliad* in this quieter manner is the episode of Hector and his infant son near the end of the sixth book. I shall again quote first the prose rendering of Lang, Leaf, and Myers, though I hope that some of my readers will turn directly to the Greek.

> So spake glorious Hector, and stretched out his arm to his boy. But the child shrunk crying to the bosom of his fair-girdled nurse, dismayed at his dear father's aspect, and in dread at the bronze and horse-hair crest that he beheld nodding fiercely from the helmet's top. Then his dear father laughed aloud, and his lady mother; forthwith glorious Hector took the helmet from his head, and laid it, all gleaming, upon the earth; then kissed he his dear son and dandled him in his arms, and spake in prayer to Zeus and all the gods, "O Zeus and all ye gods, vouchsafe ye that this my son may likewise prove even as I, pre-eminent amid the Trojans, and as valiant in might, and be a great King of Ilios. Then may men say of him, 'Far greater is he than his father' as he returneth home from battle; and may he bring with him blood-stained spoils from the foeman he hath slain, and may his mother's heart be glad." (VI, 466-81)

Pope's own "observation" on this passage (Vol. II, pp. 517-18) shows that he realized wherein its power lies: "All these are but small circumstances, but so

artfully chosen, that every Reader immediately feels
the force of them, and represents the whole in the
utmost Liveliness to his Imagination." But in his
translation he has thought necessary to overlay these
"small circumstances" with a needless prettiness of
phrasing:

> Thus having spoke, th' illustrious Chief of *Troy*
> Stretch'd his fond Arms to clasp the lovely Boy.
> The Babe clung crying to his Nurse's Breast,
> Scar'd at the dazzling Helm, and nodding Crest.
> With secret Pleasure each fond Parent smil'd,
> And *Hector* hasted to relieve his Child,
> The glitt'ring Terrors from his Brows unbound,
> And plac'd the beaming Helmet on the Ground.
> Then kist the Child, and lifting high in Air,
> Thus to the Gods prefer'd a Father's Pray'r.
> O Thou! whose Glory fills th' Ætherial Throne,
> And all ye deathless Pow'rs! protect my Son!
> Grant him, like me, to purchase just Renown,
> To guard the *Trojans*, to defend the Crown,
> Against his Country's Foes the War to wage,
> And rise the *Hector* of the future Age!
> So when triumphant from successful Toils,
> Of Heroes slain he bears the reeking Spoils,
> Whole Hosts may hail him with deserv'd Acclaim,
> And say, This Chief transcends his Father's Fame;
> While pleas'd amidst the general Shouts of *Troy*,
> His Mother's conscious Heart o'erflows with Joy.
>
> (VI, 594-615)

It is such a passage as this that justifies Warton's
criticism that the translation is "overloaded with im-
proper and unnecessary ornaments,"[12] and Johnson's
concession that there are "many Ovidian graces not
exactly suitable to Homer's character." I suppose

that to readers of the year 1716 such phrases as "glitt'ring Terrors," "prefer'd a Father's Pray'r," and "His Mother's conscious Heart" may have been more acceptable than they can be to us; but even contemporary readers, if they knew the Greek, recognized that they are not Homer. Warton records that he had been informed that "Atterbury, being in company with Bentley and Pope, insisted upon knowing the Doctor's opinion of the English Homer; and that, being earnestly pressed to declare his sentiments freely, he said, 'The verses are good verses, but the work is not Homer, it is *Spondanus.*' "[13]

The verdict of the great Dr. Bentley, most learned Grecian of his generation, rephrased as "A pretty poem, Mr. Pope; but you mustn't call it Homer,"[14] has become one of the most familiar commonplaces of criticism. Fielding echoes it in his *Amelia* (1751): Captain Booth, having been asked by a fellow prisoner of literary pretentions if he does not think Pope's Homer "the best translation in the world," replies that "though it is certainly a noble paraphrase, and of itself a fine poem, yet in some places it is no translation at all" (Book VIII, Chapter V). Thirty years later Dr. Johnson, in his Life of Pope (1781), is forced to admit that there is some truth in the charge that "Pope's version of Homer is not Homerical," but he none the less acclaims it as "a poetical wonder," "a performance which no age or nation can pretend to equal":

> To a thousand cavils one answer is sufficient; the purpose of a writer is to be read. . . . Pope wrote for

his own age and his own nation: he knew that it was
necessary to colour the images and point the sentiments of his author; he therefore made him graceful,
but lost him some of his sublimity.

Those who have repeated Bentley's verdict have
not always, like Dr. Johnson, done justice to the
poetical virtues of Pope's Homer. Too often they have
put sole emphasis on the second member of Bentley's
sentence, and have forgotten that even he admitted
that it is "a pretty poem."[15]

If Pope has in certain particulars falsified the
poetical qualities of his original, he has at least produced an English poem that one can still read with
zest, a poem that has energy and life, that glows with
that "spirit and fire" which Pope declared to be
Homer's "chief character." And it is, I think, the
only verse translation of Homer—perhaps the only
verse translation into English of any long poem—of
which so much can be said. I find Chapman's Homer,
with its Elizabethan mannerisms and its clumsy
seven-stress lines, farther from the spirit of the original than is Pope's, and as an English poem much less
readable. Our greatest debt to Chapman's Homer is
that it inspired Keats's famous sonnet. Cowper's
heavily Miltonic version of Homer is utterly impossible. Matthew Arnold in his somewhat magisterial
lectures *On Translating Homer* (1861) has enumerated
four qualities of Homer's poetry which a translator
must seek to reproduce: Homer is eminently rapid; he
is plain and direct in expression, and in the substance

of his thought; he is eminently noble. It is in plainness and directness of expression that Arnold finds Pope chiefly deficient; he grants to him rapidity and nobility and directness of thought—though with a difference.

If to the more judicious readers of Pope's own century his translation seemed to falsify some of the qualities of its original, it is inevitable that for us today the falsification should be appreciably increased. The passage of two centuries of changing literary fashions has given to Pope's diction a certain flavour of artistic obsolescence. Words and phrases which were the familiar and unnoticed currency of Augustan verse—words like "social" and "genial," or such a line as "With haste to meet him sprung the joyful Fair" (VI, 492)—savour of the drawing rooms of Hampton Court rather than of the towers of Ilium. The associations evoked by such words may heighten the pleasure with which we look at Pope's Belinda; but they do not consort so well with Homer's Andromache. And Pope's heroic couplets, though most skillfully varied and most musically modulated, are not for our taste today the appropriate equivalent of the heroic hexameter of Homer.

Could we forget that we are reading a rendering of Homer, and pretend that Pope's brilliant and swift-moving verse is singing his own Augustan tale of Troy, as Tennyson has given us a frankly Victorian recreation of Arthur's Camelot, all might be well. But such forgetting and pretending is, of course, impossible. If we mustn't call it Homer, neither can we call it altogether Pope; "Pope's Homer" is neither Homer nor Pope. It can well be maintained that of all verse translations of Homer, Pope's is the most poetical, the most readable; but the modern reader, innocent of Greek, who wishes to get what he can of Homer's art will probably turn not to any of the verse translations but to the cadenced prose of Messrs. Lang, Leaf, and Myers. And the reader who wishes to know the art of Pope will read first the *Rape of the Lock*, the *Dunciad*, the *Epistle to Dr. Arbuthnot*, and may perhaps be content with the three or four fine passages from "Homer" included in such an anthology as Mr. D. Nichol Smith's *Oxford Book of Eighteenth-Century Verse*. The Cambridge edition of Pope published by Houghton Mifflin Company is, so far as I am aware, the only edition "complete" enough to include the translations of Homer.

Though present-day readers of Pope are likely to overlook his translation of Homer, its influence on English poetry of the eighteenth century was very great indeed. It was largely through it that he left his impress, for good and for evil, on the poetry of his own generation and of the generation immediately following, particularly when that poetry chose to concern itself with more exalted themes. Pope's original poems could serve as model only for what neo-classic criticism regarded as the "lower" flights of verse—the didactic and satiric, which border on the cooler regions of prose, the pastoral and elegiac, which are but "lesser" orders of poetry. But the heroic epic is at the very top of the hierarchy, and Homer is indisputably in the grand manner. Here are nineteen thousand lines of perfectly turned heroic couplets on a high heroic theme, in poetic language that is never commonplace and is often noble. Where better could an ambitious young poet learn his craft, unless he preferred the more austere school of Milton? In either school he would learn a highly elaborated style rather than a style of simple directness; and the result was not good for English poetry. The mediocre, or less than mediocre, poet found it too easy to assume a spurious "elevation" and to echo a borrowed melody.

The more objectionable aspects of that "elevated diction" against which Wordsworth was to protest—the easy personification of abstract qualities, such heavy Latinisms as obscure the fine poetic vision of Thomson's *Seasons*, the elegant paraphrases which make sheep over into the "bleating kind" and fish into the "scaly breed"—of these Pope is only rarely guilty either in his own poetry or in his translations. The wide currency of these literary vices is due to the imitation of Milton rather than of Pope. The vocabulary of Pope's verse is not appreciably more "elevated" than that of his prose.[16] It is not so much in the choice of words as in the patterns of his style that he misled his imitators. Balance and antithesis are too neatly turned; every noun must lean upon a qualifying adjective.

Sixty years after the *Iliad* was completed, Dr. Johnson had this to say of its influence on English poetry:

> He cultivated our language with so much diligence and art, that he has left in his *Homer* a treasure of poetical elegances to posterity. His version may be said to have tuned the English tongue; for since its appearance no writer, however deficient in other powers, has wanted melody.

A treasure-mine of "poetical elegances" and of musically modulated verse is a perilous inheritance for poets "deficient in other powers" who fall heir to it. Pope could bequeath to his imitators some of his discoveries in poetic technique; he could not bequeath those burning energies of mind and spirit which make of his *Iliad*—however un-Homerical—a brilliant poetic achievement.

Pope's "Homer" brought him an independent fortune, and in his own generation enhanced his prestige as a poet; but, with all its brilliant qualities, it adds for readers of today little, if at all, to Pope's poetic stature. What that stature might have been had all the energies which were spent on Homer been directed to themes that he could have made essentially his own, it would be idle speculation to try to guess. Would Milton's poetical fame have been higher had there been no Civil War to interrupt as, after a different fashion, the ten-years' War of Troy interrupted Mr. Pope? We must be content to take our poets as we find them.

VI

THE DUNCIAD OF 1729

I

IN THE early spring of the year 1729 there was, we may be sure, one topic which monopolized conversation wherever wits and men of letters met together within the liberties of London and Westminster. Coffee-house and drawing room and dinner table were busily discussing a great literary *succès de scandale*, the audacious satire of the "Dunciad Variorum with the Prolegomena of Scriblerus." For those who found themselves pilloried in its pages it could not have been a pleasant book to read. For their friends there was, no doubt, a mixture of emotions—that not unpleasant mingling of indignant sympathy and malicious glee with which we greet the discomfiture of our associates. For the generality of readers there was provided a savoury dish compounded of brilliant and ingenious wit, subtle irony, terse epigram and spicy scandal, the whole served up with the poignant sauce of vigorous and highly wrought satiric verse. Mr. Pope from his quiet home at Twickenham delightedly watched the success of his venture. There was, to be sure, a serious purpose in his book—to save the good estate of letters and of learning, to which he bore devoted allegiance, from the depredations of pretentious dullards—but it was also a magnificent jest.

Though every one was talking about the book, not every one was lucky enough to have seen it. When the handsome quarto first made its appearance, the possession of a copy was something of an achievement; and the publication was surrounded with much mystery. The title page declared that the volume was "Printed for A. Dod"; but in strict literal fact no such bookseller existed. There had been, however, a bookseller named A. *Dodd*, whose widow was still carrying on the business under his name; and under this imprint had appeared the "imperfect" editions of the *Dunciad* which had come out in the preceding year. Technically the publishers were three powerful noblemen, good friends of Mr. Pope: Lord Bathurst, the Earl of Oxford, the Earl of Burlington—an arrangement no doubt suggested as precaution against a possible action for libel. At first copies could be obtained only on the order of one of these noblemen.

The book was first publicly vended on April 10. Before April 12 the title had been transferred to Lawton Gilliver, who entered it in the Stationers' Register on that date, and on April 17 exposed for sale a new octavo edition under his own imprint, "at Homer's Head, against St. Dunstan's Church, Fleet-street."[1]

Pope's name did not appear upon the title page;[2] but there was no attempt to conceal his authorship. The preface to the 1728 edition had contained a very broad hint; the Variorum edition makes it plain on almost every page that the anonymous "Author" of the *Dunciad* was also the author of *An Essay on Criticism* and of the translation of the *Iliad*. And, of course, no one was in the slightest doubt about the matter. It is just possible that the anonymity was sufficient to serve as some slight protection in case of a suit for libel; it could have been no protection whatever against any other sort of retaliation. To any candid reader it must be plain that the anonymous publication, and all the paraphernalia of mystery, was not a subterfuge of cowardice but a part of the jest, a mere literary device. The learned "Martinus Scriblerus" could more appropriately expend his scholarly comment on a work of unknown authorship which had previously appeared only in "imperfect" editions.

In the spring of 1729, Pope was just completing his forty-first year, and was at the height of his intellectual power. For more than a decade he had been recognized as the leading poet of his generation. His translations of Homer had not only enhanced his reputation, but had brought him a modest but sufficient fortune, with which he had established himself in independent comfort in his charming suburban villa at Twickenham, where his visitors included both the witty and the great. He had won fame and fortune by his own unaided efforts in the face of the terrible disability of his physical deformity, and the vexatious prohibitions which the law prescribed against an avowed adherent of the Roman Church. Estopped by his religion from any easy office under the government or any pension on the civil list, he had kept himself equally independent of any noble patron. He was—

> Unplaced, unpension'd, no man's heir or slave.[3]

The *Dunciad* breathes in every line and in every ironic comment the confident security of assured success, and the easy vigour of an artist who has by years of practice perfected his medium, but who is still at the peak of his intellectual power. It bears upon it the indubitable impress of genius.

The plan of his satire had been long abrewing in Pope's mind, and had been much discussed among such close friends as Swift and Gay and Bolingbroke. There is clear evidence that the poem was already partly written as early as the autumn of 1725. But Pope was in no hurry to publish the *Dunciad*; he apparently thought it wise to make a reconnaissance in force before launching his main attack on the Dunces. On March 8, 1728, appeared *The Last Volume* of the *Miscellanies* of Pope and Swift.[4] The most important piece included in the collection was Pope's prose essay *Peri Bathous, Or The Art of Sinking in Poetry*, a deliciously witty piece of sustained irony in which are given grave instructions for the writing of dull poetry. Longinus had written his treatise "Of the Sublime"; but, as "Martinus Scriblerus," the imaginary author of Pope's skit, informs us in his opening chapter:

> . . . no Track has been yet chalk'd out, to arrive at our Βάθος or *profund*. . . . Wherefore considering with no small Grief, how many promising

Genius's of this Age are wandering (as I may say) in
the dark without a Guide, I have undertaken this
arduous but necessary Task, to lead them as it were
by the hand, and step by step, the gentle downhill way
to the Bathos; the Bottom, the End, the Central
Point, the *non plus ultra*, of true Modern Poesie!

The satire is pointed by copious illustrations from
bad poets. The chief victims of Pope's irony are Sir
Richard Blackmore, author of interminable epics,
"The Father of the *Bathos*, and indeed the *Homer* of
it,"[5] and Mr. Ambrose Philips; but Chapter VI, "Of
the Several Kinds of Genius's in the *Profund*, and the
Marks and Characters of Each," contains under the
thin veil of easily deciphered initials a broadside of
ridicule directed against the writings of the less-than-
minor poets who are also ridiculed in the *Dunciad*, a
broadside which promptly drew, as Pope had anticipated, a return fire from the "sundry and manifold
choice spirits in this our island" who found themselves
classified as the "Porpoises," the "Frogs" or the
"Eels" of poetry. For the next two months the weekly
journals were filled with abusive attacks on Mr.
Pope.[6] The Dunces had fallen into his trap, and had
given him the provocation which he desired as justification for his grand attack.

It was now time to publish the poem, and on May
18 there appeared a slender volume of some sixty
pages, to be had either in duodecimo or in octavo,[7]
with the title: "The Dunciad. An Heroic poem. In
Three Books.—Dublin, Printed, London Reprinted
for A. Dodd. 1728." The frontispiece is a morose owl

perched on a pedestal of books—the writings of Cibber, the Duchess of Newcastle, Dennis, Ogilby, Blackmore, and Theobald's *Shakespeare Restored*. There is a six-page preface, "The Publisher to the Reader"; and the text is accompanied by a few brief footnotes. The names of the Dunces are not printed in full, but are indicated by first and last letters with intervening dashes. Though Pope's authorship is not openly acknowledged, it is broadly hinted in the Publisher's preface.

This vagueness as to authorship, and the misleading words of the title page which imply that the volume was "reprinted" from an earlier impression at Dublin —for which there was not the slightest basis in fact— were dictated not by any desire of concealment, but by purely literary considerations. Pope was clearly seeking to enhance the effect of his satire by surrounding it with an air of mystery and conjecture, as the work of a nameless author in the far-away city of Dublin. As concealment, save as it may have served to keep Pope on the windy side of the law of libel, it would have been but a clumsy pretence; but as artistic illusion it was admirable—for, as Pope well knew, the illusion of art is quite independent of reasonable belief.

It was not, then, until Pope had prepared its way with much elaboration of stratagem, and had created for it a highly effective stage-setting of secrecy and mystification, that he permitted the world to see in the early spring of 1729, in its "complete" and "per-

fect" form, "The Dunciad Variorum with the Prolegomena of Scriblerus." He had, to borrow the words
of the "Advertisement," seen to it that his satire
should "partake of the nature of a *Secret*, which most
people love to be let into."

The "complete" and "perfect" *Dunciad* of 1729 had
become a substantial volume of 172 pages. The poem
itself was longer by nearly a hundred lines, and there
was the added bulk of Prolegomena, Remarks, and
Appendices. The names of the Dunces, which in 1728
had been indicated by initials, were now with a few
exceptions printed out in full. The vigour of Pope's
satire and its inherent interest for the contemporary
public, together with the elaborate mystifications
with which Pope had ushered it into the world, were
sufficient to insure it a host of readers. During the
year 1729 the book appeared in a variety of issues, in
quarto and octavo, at London and at Dublin.

II

From the beginning, one of the objections most frequently urged against the *Dunciad* by hostile critics
has been the insignificance of its victims, that they
were utterly unworthy of the energy of attack which
Pope has expended on them. The Dunces, we have
been told, are but butterflies broken on the wheel of
needlessly vigorous satire; they have acquired from
Pope's very attack the only immortality for which
they could ever reasonably have hoped. Even when
the satire was little more than a project in the poet's

mind, Swift had written warningly to his friend on
November 26, 1725:

> Take care the bad poets do not outwit you, as they
> have served the good ones in every age, whom they
> have provoked to transmit their names to posterity.
> Mævius is as well known as Virgil, and Gildon will
> be as well known as you, if his name gets into your
> verses. . . .

In the "Letter to the Publisher" prefixed to the edition of 1729 and signed by William Cleland—though
written, we may more than guess, by Pope himself—
one reads: "The first objection I have heard made to
the Poem is, that the persons are too obscure for
Satyre." The modern reader, who must learn from
the weary perusal of many footnotes who and what
most of the Dunces were, is more than likely to echo
the objection.

A nineteenth-century critic of the poem—but one
who writes of Pope with a virulence of dislike not unworthy of a contemporary enemy—has urged quite
the opposite objection. Professor Lounsbury, in
Chapter XIV of his book rather misleadingly entitled
The Text of Shakespeare, has undertaken to show that
Pope's victims, if not quite to be regarded as "great
and good men," were at least persons of some considerable importance in their own day:

> The truth is that nearly all the writers satirized in
> "The Dunciad" had either distinguished themselves
> or were to distinguish themselves in some particular
> field of intellectual effort. The position they held in
> the eyes of the public furnishes presumptive proof
> that they were not dunces. (pp. 259-60)

And Lounsbury continues through many pages to
show that, whatever their shortcomings, the persons
of the *Dunciad* were not fools and imbeciles, and that
despite Pope's attack they continued to flourish and
prosper. We may grant at once his contention that
Pope's victims were not insignificant nobodies; but it
is plain that Lounsbury had not stopped in his zeal of
rehabilitation to ask himself in what sense of the word
Pope was using the term "dunce."

It is a word with a curious history behind it.
Originally it is the extension of a proper name, that
of one of the great masters of scholastic philosophy,
Duns Scotus. In the days when the triumph of the new
humanism had thrown into utter disrepute the philosophy of the medieval schoolmen, the name *Duns*
was applied to any exponent of this discredited discipline. With the humanists of the sixteenth century
it had taken on the sense of "cavilling sophist," "hair-
splitting pedant." As Pope uses the word, it suggests
not stupidity or ignorance, but a perverse misapplica-
tion of intelligence, learning without wisdom, the
precise opposite of all that is implied by the term
"humanist."

The character of the "dunce" is not imbecility but
dulness; and "dull," as Pope uses the word, is the
direct opposite of "enlightened" and "enlightening."
This is made clear by a note to line 15 of Book I, first
added in the edition of 1743:

> I wonder the learned Scriblerus has omitted to ad-
> vertise the Reader, at the opening of this Poem, that
> Dulness here is not to be taken contractedly for mere

> Stupidity, but in the enlarged sense of the word, for all
> Slowness of Apprehension, Shortness of Sight, or im-
> perfect Sense of things. It includes (as we see by the
> Poet's own words) Labour, Industry, and some degree
> of Activity and Boldness; a ruling principle not inert,
> but turning topsy-turvy the Understanding, and in-
> ducing an Anarchy or confused State of Mind.

Mr. Courthope has summed up the matter excellently
by saying: "in the word 'Dulness,' Pope meant to
include every sort of rebellion against right reason
and good taste."[8]

Lounsbury was quite right in his assertion that
many of the Dunces were in their own day persons
of some consequence in the world of letters. The Rev.
Laurence Eusden, the "parson much bemused in
beer,"[9] was Poet Laureate from 1719 until his death
in 1730, when he was succeeded by another of the
Dunces, Colley Cibber. But with few exceptions these
important personages of two centuries ago are of very
little interest to any one today.

If Pope has chosen with extraordinary critical pre-
vision the authors whom he should lampoon, he has
been equally happy in those whom he singled out for
praise. In a note to II, 132, we read:

> Nothing is more remarkable than our author's love
> of praising good writers. He has celebrated Sir *Isaac
> Newton*, Mr. *Dryden*, Mr. *Congreve*, Mr. *Wycherley*,
> Dr. *Garth*, Mr. *Walsh*, Duke of *Buckingham*, Mr.
> *Addison*, Lord *Lansdown*; in a word, almost every
> man of his time that deserv'd it.

Of the nine names included in this list only three
would seem to modern readers undeserving of much

praise. To the list Pope might have added the names of Swift and Gay and Prior. Edward Young, who was in 1729 known only as the author of a brilliant set of verse satires, *The Love of Fame* (1725), appears among Pope's friends in the "Testimonies of Authors"; James Thomson, whose *Seasons* in their completed form did not appear till 1730, is no where mentioned in the *Dunciad*. He and Pope were very shortly to become fast friends.

If it be objected that the persons praised are Pope's personal friends, and the Dunces his personal enemies, the objector must at least admit that Pope chose his friends remarkably well. Among their number are included nearly all of his contemporaries whom we today care to remember. We may judge a man by his friends—and almost equally by the quality of those who were his foes.

III

As the grave and learned Martinus Scriblerus has taken pains to inform the reader in his discourse "Of the Poem," the *Dunciad* is an epic poem, but an epic of the comic rather than the tragic order, seeking its classical precedent and model not in the *Iliad* or the *Æneid* but in the lost Homeric *Margites*, which "was properly and absolutely a *Dunciad*." Judged merely as mock-heroic, the *Dunciad* in most particulars falls below the exquisite artistry of the *Rape of the Lock*. The earlier poem is delicate and delicious parody; the *Dunciad* is broad (and sometimes indecent) burlesque. If the dominant character of the *Rape* is sparkling wit and playful fancy, the *Dunciad* is marked by its amazing vigour and buoyancy of spirit.

The *Rape of the Lock*, magnificent trifle though it is, has a single and unified mock-heroic action. Never does the reader forget through its varied episodes— the game of ombre, the great battle of Hampton Court, the descent to the Cave of Spleen, the delicate ministry of Ariel and his sylphs—the central theme of Belinda's ravished lock. The *Dunciad* has no such informing unity of structure. Scriblerus tells us (pp. 24-5) that:

> The Action of the Dunciad is the Removal of the Imperial seat of Dulness from the City to the polite world; as that of the Æneid is the Removal of the empire of *Troy* to *Latium*. . . . The *Fable* being thus according to best example one and entire, as contain'd in the proposition; the *Machinery* is a continued chain of Allegories, setting forth the whole power, ministry, and empire of Dulness, extended thro' her subordinate instruments, in all her various operations. This is branched into *Episodes*, each of which hath its Moral apart, tho' all conducive to the main end.

But the "one and entire" action, the overthrow of polite and humane learning, is all but lost in the branching episodes. It is the "continued chain of Allegories," the satire on false taste in literature and learning, which constitutes the essential unity of the *Dunciad*, a unity admirably maintained in the tone of scornful contempt which runs through the whole. The burlesque epic form is but the subordinate minister of the satire; we have the paraphernalia of the epic—

heroic games, a descent to the lower world, a prophetic vision or "Pisgah-sight" of the future—rather than the substance of the heroic poem. And, since the critical apparatus of prolegomena and comment and learned appendix is an essential part of the satire, the *Dunciad* as a whole is a burlesque of pedantic scholarship quite as much as it is burlesque epic. The essentially comic spirit of the *Rape of the Lock*, with at most a playful satire on the foibles of fashionable society in general, makes possible a formal unity which in the more ambitious, and more serious, *Dunciad* gives place to a unity of spirit and satiric purpose.

The satire of the *Dunciad* is at the same time general and intensely personal. It is Pope's aim "to correct the taste of the town in wit and criticism," and to set in the pillory of his scornful humour the individual Dunces who are the embodiments for the moment of all the tendencies that make against good taste and humane learning. Pope has insisted that the personal element in his satire is subordinate to the general. In the address of "The Publisher to the Reader," which prefaced the "imperfect" editions of 1728, and was reprinted as Appendix I to the edition of 1729, the reader is informed:

> For whoever will consider the Unity of the whole design, will be sensible, that the *Poem was not made for these Authors, but these Authors for the Poem*: And I should judge they were clapp'd in as they rose, fresh and fresh, and chang'd from day to day, in like manner as when the old boughs wither, we thrust new ones into a chimney. (p. 90)

It is true, indeed, that in the successive editions of the poem Pope changed in many a passage the personal exemplifications of his satire, clapping in fresh victims as the old ones withered in their importance. Since we know that the poem was projected and partly written some months before the publication of *Shakespeare Restored*, it is clear that it was not originally devised merely for the humiliation of Lewis Theobald; but how far we should take at its face value the assertion that the personalities are merely incidental to the general purpose is a question on which there is room for difference of opinion.

Editors and critics have usually emphasized the personal lampoons almost to the utter neglect of the more general satire, and have conveyed the idea that the *Dunciad* is but the expression of Pope's personal animosity against those who had wounded his pride by attacks upon him—real, or merely imagined by his inflamed sensitiveness. Commentators have busied themselves to explain in the case of each person pilloried the particular provocation which called forth the resentment of the "wasp of Twickenham," and to discuss, often in a spirit hostile to Pope, the question as to who was in truth the first aggressor. And modern readers have in consequence not unnaturally assumed that, without a minute acquaintance with all these forgotten personalities, they could not hope to understand the poem. Pope realized that even to his contemporaries many of his Dunces would be but unknown names. In the preface to the edition of 1728, where the names were not printed in full, but merely indicated by first and final letters, the "Publisher" says:

> I would not have the reader too much troubled or anxious, if he cannot decypher them; since when he shall have found them out, he will probably know no more of the Persons than before.

Just how far this is to be taken ironically as merely a further disparagement of the Dunces, how far as literal truth, it is not easy to say. If it was true in 1728, it is incomparably truer for the reader of two centuries later. Though we are presented with the names in full rather than with initials and dashes, the task of "finding out" the persons is accomplished only by much weary reading of commentaries; and, when all the notes have been read, the names have at best been metamorphosed into shadows. Like the contending booksellers of Book II, we grasp at phantom poets. Most readers of today will best appreciate the *Dunciad* by keeping its general significance in mind, and regarding the individual Dunces as types rather than individuals. They may even amuse themselves by substituting for these forgotten persons of long ago their own pet aversions in the literary world of the present. The crisp and racy annotations of the Variorum edition are usually sufficient to explain the point of the satire; though one must at times disentangle fact from irony, and must never forget that they are far removed from impartial fairness. They are, of course, part and parcel of the satire itself.

Pope himself is in no small measure responsible for the idea that his satire is but the fruit of personal resentment. He has given us in the "Testimonies of Authors," in the "List of Books, Papers, and Verses, in which our Author was abused," in the "Parallel of the Characters of Mr. Dryden and Mr. Pope," and in many of the footnotes, his proof—not in all cases quite ingenuous—that the Dunces had been the first aggressors, that he is attacking only those who had themselves attacked him in his person and his writings. It is quite plain that he felt that he must guard himself against the charge of wanton aggression.

That against some of the Dunces Pope did cherish deep resentment, and that wounded pride has added venom to the shafts of his satire, no one can deny; but the *Dunciad* is not merely, nor I think mainly, the record of personal animosity. Its prevailing tone is one of contempt rather than of anger. In none of its attacks does one catch the note of exasperated bitterness which marks the portrait of Lord Hervey in the famous "Sporus" passage of the *Epistle to Dr. Arbuthnot*. Those of his biographers who have pictured Pope as a creature of inflamed sensitiveness, writhing in agony under the attack of men indisputably his inferiors in literary talent and in social station, and hitting out at them in mere exasperation, have, I think, greatly exaggerated the truth. A sensitive man, always painfully conscious of his physical deformity, Pope undoubtedly was. But he was also a man of fearless courage, neither himself a flatterer of the great, nor more than most human beings easily to be flattered.

In all of the correspondence between Pope and his
friends which has to do with the *Dunciad*, before and
after its publication, one finds an exuberance of good
spirits rather than the exasperation of wounded feel-
ings. No one can read the satire without a sense of the
zest of battle, the sheer delight in the audacity of the
undertaking, the overflowing ingenuity of attack.
Though there is a serious purpose in it all, it is carried
through in the light-hearted spirit of a magnificent
jest.

In his satire first published in 1738 under the title
"One Thousand Seven Hundred and Thirty Eight,"
which later became the *Epilogue to the Satires*, Pope
has given his own version of the matter:

> Ask you what provocation I have had?
> The strong Antipathy of Good to Bad.

He is not here speaking particularly of the *Dunciad*,
but in general of his use of the "sacred weapon" of
satire. Whatever may be Pope's shortcomings, however much he may have deviated at times from the
paths of straightforward dealing, no attentive reader
of his poetry can doubt the genuineness of his "strong
antipathy" to bad writing, and to all the pretentious
enemies of an enlightened and humane civilization,
who seemed to him to be corrupting the taste of his
age. Whatever of personal animosity may be present
in the *Dunciad*, this "strong antipathy" is the dominant motive. Once more the reader must remember
that with very few exceptions the persons whom
Pope has impaled were really *bad* writers, and, within
the special meaning which he attaches to the term,

deserving of the name of Dunce. If at times the satire seems to us to overstep the limits of good taste in the virulence of its personal attack, Pope was but following the custom of his time. The satire of the Augustan age was no respecter of persons.

IV

To Pope and to the whole circle of his friends—to Swift and Gay and Dr. Arbuthnot—it seemed that the fine fabric of humane learning, and of the art of writing as its chief exponent, was being torn to rags and tatters by certain evil tendencies which were every day gaining in strength and in blatant self-confidence. There had been in the early decades of the eighteenth century a sudden and enormous increase in the size of the reading public. Literature was now the concern not of the chosen few but of the indiscriminate many. To borrow the words of Scriblerus (p. 23), Pope "lived in those days, when (after providence had permitted the Invention of Printing as a scourge for the Sins of the learned) Paper also became so cheap, and printers so numerous, that a deluge of authors cover'd the land."

Among these enemies of sound learning and good taste come first and foremost this "deluge of authors," the whole tribe of Grub-street, bad poets, dull writers, literary hacks:

> Some strain in rhyme; the Muses, on their racks,
> Scream, like the winding of ten thousand Jacks:
> Some free from rhyme or reason, rule or check,
> Break Priscian's head, and Pegasus's neck.   (III, 153-6)

Their mercenary allies are the booksellers, or as we
should call them the publishers, who were concerned,
Pope thought, not to sponsor good writing, but merely
to make their profit out of pandering to a corrupt
popular taste, who, slow to recognize real merit, vied
with one another to publish all that was pretentiously
cheap, scurrilous, and low. And with them rank bad
critics, encouragers of dull writing, and the noble
patrons who were to be bought by the tickling
flattery of a dedication. A separate category is formed
by the "Party-writers," whether Whig or Tory, whose
chief qualifications are "to stick at nothing, to delight
in flinging dirt, and to slander in the dark by guess,"
and whose vehicles are the "weekly journals"—
"papers of news and scandal intermix'd, on different
sides and parties and frequently shifting from one
side to the other."[10]

As the booksellers cater only to the depraved taste
of the many, so the theatres give to the public not the
great art of drama, but mere spectacle and noise—
farce and pantomime, and that pet aversion of all the
Queen Anne wits, Italian opera with all its impassioned absurdity of *aria* and *recitativo*. To Pope it
seemed the crowning objection to these perversions of
dramatic art that they had ceased to hold the mirror
up to Nature, and moved instead in "a new world to
Nature's laws unknown":

> He look'd, and saw a sable Sorc'rer rise,
> Swift to whose hand a winged volume flies:
> All sudden, Gorgons hiss, and Dragons glare,
> And ten-horn'd fiends and Giants rush to war.
> Hell rises, Heav'n descends, and dance on Earth,

Gods, imps, and monsters, music, rage, and mirth,
A fire, a jig, a battle, and a ball,
Till one wide Conflagration swallows all.

(III, 229-36)

If one takes into account the whole of the "Dunciad Variorum" with its prolegomena, its "remarks," its appendices and indices, probably the chief thrust of the satire is directed against the dull pedantry of the textual critics, as embodied in the fictitious person of Martinus Scriblerus. To all of Pope's circle of friends pedantry was the deadliest of sins. "Scriblerus" had been the playful joint invention of Swift and Pope and Parnell and the brilliant group of wits who had met during the last year of Queen Anne's reign in the rooms of the gracious and gifted Dr. Arbuthnot. They were busy devising for him a biography and a set of learned "memoirs," when the death of the Queen and the fall of the Tory ministry scattered the members of the "Scriblerus Club" and brought their satirical project to an end. "The design of the Memoirs of Scriblerus was to have ridiculed all the false tastes in learning, under the character of a man of capacity enough; that had dipped into every art and science, but injudiciously in each."[11] Pope had taken his name as the imaginary author of the "Bathos"; and it is he who serves as ponderous editor of the "Dunciad Variorum." As textual critic and commentator, Scriblerus stands for the type of scholarship exemplified by Richard Bentley.

Bentley was a man of vast erudition, the greatest classical scholar of his generation. To his own work, and to the tradition of which he is one of the origi-

nators, we owe the establishment of the canon, and the
recovery of accurate texts, of the ancient authors and
of the earlier monuments of modern literature. Such
work as his is the indispensable foundation of any
sound study of the literature of Greece and Rome.
Until we have separated the genuine writings of an
author from those spuriously assigned to him, and
have purged his text at least from the more serious
corruptions, we can arrive at no trustworthy knowledge of him. But without this foundation, the great
humanists of the fifteenth and sixteenth centuries had
recovered for themselves and for the world in general
the essential spirit of classical antiquity. Even from
corrupt texts they had imbibed the philosophy of
Plato, and had felt the majesty of the great poets and
orators. For Bentley and his like these greater values
of ancient literature had been all but sunk in the
details of minute scholarship. To Pope and his circle,
men bred as polite humanists rather than as exact
scholars, and filled with an undiscriminating hatred
of all "pedantry," Bentley seemed to have no sense
of values at all. One ancient author was apparently as
important to him as another—provided that there
was opportunity for "restoring" a corrupted text.
And it must be owned that to this process of "restoring" Bentley applied his vast reading and accurate
knowledge in the spirit of a trained logician rather
than of a man sensitive to the qualities of great literature—qualities which are something more than logic.
If much of his work is of enduring value, as it surely is,
it must not be forgotten that a not inconsiderable

proportion of his conjectural emendations are the tasteless absurdities of logic misapplied. As Pope was to write of him and his kind in the *Epistle to Dr. Arbuthnot*:

> Pains, reading, study, are their just pretence,
> And all they want is spirit, taste, and sense.

The amusing appendix to the *Dunciad* entitled "Virgilius Restauratus" is, of course, a parody of his method; but as parody it is not unfair to that part of his work which is concerned with conjectural emendation. His own application of the method to the text of *Paradise Lost*, published in 1732, is more preposterous than any parody.[12]

The first to apply Bentley's methods to the "restoration" of the text of an English author was Lewis Theobald, whom Pope has raised to the bad eminence of King of his Dunces—and Theobald's essay in textual criticism was of a sort to bring him and his methods very vividly and very painfully to Pope's attention.

Pope, in an unhappy moment for his peace of mind and for his reputation, had undertaken in 1720 to prepare for the publisher Jacob Tonson an edition of the plays of Shakespeare. It was a task for which he was ill fitted; and his performance of it was not satisfactory, even when judged by the standards of 1725. His Preface is a noble piece of critical appreciation. His text, though he made some pretence of collating the quartos and early folios—which had not been done at all by his predecessor, Rowe—is careless and slipshod in the extreme. He brought to his work poetic taste and generous appreciation; what he lacked was the laborious scholarship of such a man as Lewis Theobald.[13]

Theobald was, curiously enough, Pope's exact contemporary. Both the poet of the *Dunciad* and its hero were born in the year 1688 and died in 1744. Though bred to his father's profession of the law, Theobald devoted his energies mainly to literature and to scholarly pursuits. The most significant of his attempts at poetry was *The Cave of Poverty* (1715), written in the six-line stanza of *Venus and Adonis*, and in avowed imitation of Shakespeare's diction. He had tried his hand, not very successfully, at drama, but had achieved considerable success in pantomime. *The Necromancer or Dr. Faustus* and *The Rape of Proserpine*, his most popular works in this kind, had been produced, with much splendour of spectacle, in 1723 and 1725 under the direction of John Rich. He had published various translations from the Greek, including one of the first books of the *Odyssey* (1717) accompanied by proposals for a translation of the entire poem, which may well have seemed to Pope a presumptuous intrusion on his own literary preserves.[14]

But Theobald's only work of permanent importance was that on the text of Shakespeare. Pope's perfunctory edition had appeared in March of 1725. Almost exactly a year later was published Theobald's "Shakespeare restored: or, A Specimen of the Many Errors as well committed, as Unamended, by Mr. Pope In his Late Edition of this Poet. Designed not only to correct the said Edition, but to restore the

True Reading of Shakespeare in all the Editions ever yet publish'd." The handsomely printed quarto of 194 pages applies to the text of Shakespeare the same method of critical examination which Bentley was using in his "restoration" of Greek and Latin texts. The main body of the book (pp. 1-132) consists of 97 textual notes on passages in *Hamlet*; an Appendix (pp. 133-94) in smaller type gives 107 miscellaneous emendations of Pope's edition in the text of the other plays.

Theobald brought to his work not only scholarly patience in collating the folios and quartos but a very considerable knowledge of Shakespearean vocabulary and grammar. Though some of the proposed emendations of a purely conjectural nature are mistaken and tasteless, others have been universally accepted; particularly happy is his famous emendation in the scene of Falstaff's death. Where the emendation consists in restoring to the text a reading from one of the early copies, Theobald is usually right. A considerable number of emendations have to do with "false pointing" in Pope's text, with misplaced commas and semicolons which obscure or distort the meaning. The most serious stricture which can be made on his work is his apparent lack of any sense of proportion. He pounces with the same correcting zeal on a mistaken punctuation as on a more material corruption. Throughout, his method is that of the triumphant logician; rarely if ever does he seem conscious, even in a passing word, of the fact that he is concerned with great poetry.

Such minute attention to the text as is involved in
Theobald's emendations is, of course, the indispensable basis of any sound and permanent criticism of a
more humane sort; but Pope and his brilliant circle of
friends, failing to recognize this, saw in it only an
illiberal and pedantic preoccupation with trifles, a
mere "word-catching," a worship of commas and
points. Pedantic in its tone and manner the book indisputably is.

Apart from *Shakespeare Restored*, Theobald would
probably have found an inconspicuous place in the
Dunciad as a mediocre poet, a book-seller's hack, and,
still worse, the author of successful pantomimes.
Pope's satire, one will remember, was already partly
written before the appearance of *Shakespeare Restored*,
so that Theobald can hardly have been originally its
central figure. By his Shakespearean emendations he
added to his other qualifications as a Dunce that of
textual criticism, and of a criticism directed explicitly against the more genial but utterly slipshod
scholarship of Pope's unhappy venture as editor of
Shakespeare. In the words of Pope's own note to I,
106, "Probably that proceeding elevated him to the
Dignity he holds in this Poem, which he seems to
deserve no other way better than his brethren."[15]

V

Though Theobald has been elevated to the dignity
of chief Dunce, and as their anointed King holds
technically the centre of the stage throughout, in

actual fact not more than two hundred of the thousand-odd lines which make up the poem are directed at him. He is but first among his brethren in dulness. It is only the first book which is primarily devoted to Theobald as the preeminent embodiment of Dulness, and so worthily crowned King of the Dunces in succession to Elkanah Settle, chief Dunce of the preceding generation—as Shadwell succeeds Flecnoe in Dryden's *MacFlecnoe*, which is in some sort the model of the *Dunciad*. The first hundred lines of the book are given to general satire on the theme of literary ineptitude. After the epic invocation and the dedication to Swift, we are shown the abode of Dulness and her throne supported by the four cardinal virtues of bad writing:

> Fierce champion Fortitude, that knows no fears
> Of hisses, blows, or want, or loss of ears:
> Calm Temperance, whose blessings those partake
> Who hunger, and who thirst, for scribling sake:
> Prudence, whose glass presents th' approaching jayl:
> Poetic Justice, with her lifted scale;
> Where in nice balance, truth with gold she weighs,
> And solid pudding against empty praise.   (I, 45-52)

We look appalled into a Miltonic chaos made up of the warring elements of bad literary art. Then, at line 106, Theobald is introduced sitting supperless[16] in the midst of his library:

> Studious he sate, with all his books around,
> Sinking from thought to thought, a vast profound!
> Plung'd for his sense, but found no bottom there;
> Then writ, and flounder'd on, in mere despair.
> (I, 111-14)

To appreciate these lines one need not know much of
Lewis Theobald. Is there any literary craftsman who
does not recognize unhappy moments of his own? or
any reader who has not wearily perused books so
written? Theobald's library is composed of two sorts
of books—his "polite learning," dull poets selected
for their binding or for their size upon his shelves;
and his "solid learning," Caxton, Wynkyn de Worde,
Philemon Holland, books of mere antiquarian interest, "the Classicks of an Age that heard of none."
He builds of these ponderous folios an altar on which
he prepares to burn his own writings. Praying to the
goddess Dulness, he tells her of his accomplishments
as textual critic:

> Here studious I unlucky moderns save,
> Nor sleeps one error in its father's grave,
> Old puns restore, lost blunders nicely seek,
> And crucify poor Shakespear once a week.[17]

(I, 161-4)

He tells of his work as a poet, inspired by "Emptiness
and Dulness," and as a "party-writer." He is about
to set fire to his own "cold" writings; but Dulness,
roused by the unfamiliar light, extinguishes the
flames, manifests herself to Theobald, and takes him
to her own abode. There, having shown to "her
chosen" all her triumphs of bad writing and shallow
learning, she crowns him King of Dunces amid the
tumultuous acclaim of all Grub-street.

Book II is entirely taken up with the episode of the
games instituted by Dulness in honour of Theobald's
coronation. Theobald watches from his throne, but

takes no part, and the satire is entirely bestowed on other victims. In the devising of these games Pope has shown an ingenuity of Rabelaisian wit which makes up in boisterous energy what it lacks in delicacy. Into it has gone some of the same delight in filth which marks the satire of his friend Swift, who in the digressions of *A Tale of a Tub* had already attacked many of the same abuses in letters and learning that inspired the *Dunciad*. One of the chief targets of lampoon is Edmund Curll, the utterly disreputable publisher, who by the aid of Cloacina wins the honour of publishing the works of the "phantom poet," James Moore-Smyth, and by a second triumph of obscenity wins also Eliza Haywood, chosen to represent "the profligate licentiousness of those shameless scriblers (for the most part of That sex, which ought least be capable of such malice or impudence) who in libellous Memoirs and Novels, reveal the faults and misfortunes of both sexes, to the ruin or disturbance, of publick fame or private happiness."[18] There is satire on noble patrons who are to be won by the tickling flattery of soft dedication, on dramatic writers who depend for their effects chiefly on noise, and on the "party-writers," whose game of diving into the mud of Fleet-ditch symbolizes the depths of nastiness to which they will descend in their favourite occupation of "flinging dirt." The last of the games is the highly ingenious contest of endurance, to see who can longest stay awake during the reading of Sir Richard Blackmore's interminable epics and the rhetorical periods of "Orator" Henley, a notorious dissenting preacher and highly successful religious charlatan.

Book III, which may well have been the germinal idea of the whole satire, is the "progress of Dulness." Theobald, put to sleep like the rest by the works of Blackmore and Henley, dreams that he has descended to "th' Elyzian shade," where on the banks of this literary Lethe poets await the birth of publication. Thence he is taken by his forerunner, Settle, up into a high hill from which he beholds in a vision the past triumphs of Dulness and, in the future, her complete victory over all that makes for intelligence. Bad poets and critics, antiquaries like Thomas Hearne, the verbal critics, "Forever reading, never to be read," charlatans in religion and free-thinking deists, writers of farce and opera, "party-writers," all the forces of Dulness are arrayed for the final day of triumph, when "universal darkness covers all." This final victory is described in lines, later transferred with slight revision to the end of the added fourth book, in which satiric verse rises to the heights of real sublimity:

> She comes! the Cloud-compelling Pow'r, behold!
> With Night Primæval, and with Chaos old.
> Lo! the great Anarch's ancient reign restor'd,
> Light dies before her uncreating word:
> As one by one, at dread Medæa's strain,
> The sick'ning Stars fade off the a'therial plain;
> As Argus' eyes, by Hermes wand opprest,
> Clos'd one by one to everlasting rest;
> Thus at her felt approach, and secret might,
> Art after Art goes out, and all is Night.   (III, 337-46)

The *Dunciad* is not only great satire, but in its kind great poetry. In none of his writings is Pope's mastery of the couplet more complete than here. Line answers line, and couplet builds on couplet, with the sure inevitability of supreme literary craftsmanship. Where the satire calls for such effects, the lines have a studied harshness or a languishing softness; their prevailing tone is one of easy vigour and light-hearted gaiety.

The *Dunciad* is great poetry not only in the music of its verse, but in its power to evoke images which carry immediate conviction, if not to the imagination in the higher meanings of that word, at least to the poetic fancy of the reader, images which with nicest accuracy embody the poet's thought. Take, for example, the following couplets, which are a playful parody of a well-known passage in Denham's *Cooper's Hill*:

> Flow, Welsted, flow! like thine inspirer, Beer,
> Tho' stale, not ripe; tho' thin, yet never clear;
> So sweetly mawkish, and so smoothly dull;
> Heady, not strong, and foaming tho' not full.

> (III, 163-6)

Or these, in which Theobald describes his methods as a textual critic:

> For thee I dim these eyes, and stuff this head,
> With all such reading as was never read;
> . . . .
> For thee explain a thing till all men doubt it,
> And write about it, Goddess, and about it;
> So spins the silkworm small its slender store,
> And labours, 'till it clouds itself all o'er.   (I, 165-72)

The images are usually, as the subject demands, grotesque rather than beautiful; but here and there we come upon such lines as:

> Lo where Mœotis sleeps, and hardly flows
> The freezing Tanais thro' a waste of Snows,
>
> (III, 79-80)

lines which haunt the imagination both by their imagery and their music.

Ordinarily the appeal is of a different sort than this, an appeal to the understanding rather than the senses. Like all poetic satire, the *Dunciad* is art of a highly intellectual cast. From the nature of its substance, it cannot often touch our sensibility or move our sympathy. It offers instead that keen joy of recognition which comes as we watch the flashing play of a disciplined mind, which is also indubitably the mind of a poet.

Pope's Dunces are long since dead and forgotten save as he has given to them an ironic immortality; the abuses which they exemplify are still, many of them, with us, though showing themselves in the changed colours of another age; but the *Dunciad* is still alive, after the lapse of two centuries, with the superb vitality of its satiric art.

VII

MORALIZED SONG

I

WHEN in the *Epistle to Dr. Arbuthnot* Pope reviews his career as a poet, he accounts it a merit—

> That not in Fancy's maze he wander'd long,
> But stoop'd to Truth, and moraliz'd his song. (340-1)

By his wanderings in the maze of Fancy, he means, I take it, such pieces as the *Pastorals*, the *Rape of the Lock*, the *Unfortunate Lady*, and *Eloisa to Abelard*; by "moralized song," he clearly intends such poems as the *Essay on Man*, the *Moral Essays*, and his Horatian satires. The word "stooped" is a metaphor from the sport of falconry. From the airy heights of fancy, or imagination, the confused mists of unreality, he descended like a clear-eyed bird of prey to seize on the quarry of sober truth, the world of actual men and women, with its problems of thought and conduct, its manners and morals, its *mores*. Epistle IV of the *Moral Essays*, "Of Taste," was published in December of 1731; for the remaining years of Pope's life, his poetic activity was to exercise itself all but exclusively in those less exalted regions of the Aonian mount which are the domain of satire and didactic verse.

In June, 1729, while the triumphant *Dunciad* was still fresh in everyone's mind, Fenton wrote to Broome:

I saw our friend Pope twice when I was at London.
. . . The war is carried on against him furiously in
pictures and libels . . . He told me that for the future he
intended to write nothing but epistles in Horace's
manner, in which I question not but he will succeed
very well.[1]

In the deliberate choice of this poetic province, Pope
may have been influenced by his close friend, Lord
Bolingbroke. In November, 1729, two full years before
the publication of the *Moral Essay* "Of Taste,"
Bolingbroke wrote to Swift:

Bid him [Pope] talk to you of the work he is about,
I hope in good earnest. It is a fine one; and will be,
in his hands, an original. His sole complaint is, that
he finds it too easy in the execution. This flatters his
laziness. It flatters my judgment, who always thought
that, universal as his talents are, this is eminently and
peculiarly his, above all the writers I know, living or
dead: I do not except Horace.

And in a letter from Pope to Swift which went to
Ireland under the same cover, Pope explains:

The work he [Bolingbroke] speaks of with such
abundant partiality is a system of ethics in the Horatian way.

In the concluding paragraph of the *Essay on Man*
Pope says, addressing his "guide, philosopher, and
friend":

urg'd by thee, I turn'd the tuneful art
From sounds to things, from fancy to the heart;
For Wit's false mirror held up Nature's light.

(IV, 391-3)

Pope's cultivation of this new field came to most
abundant harvest in the years 1733 and 1734 and the

early weeks of 1735.² On January 15, 1733, was published the *Moral Essay*, "Of Riches"; a month later, February 15, appeared the first of the Horatian satires, the "First Satire of the Second Book of Horace," *To Mr. Fortescue*. These poems bore Pope's name on the title page. Five days after the Horatian imitation (February 20) was published anonymously, by a book-seller not previously associated with Pope, the first epistle of the *Essay on Man*, followed in March and May by the second and third epistles. By publishing two acknowledged pieces in the weeks just preceding, Pope succeeded in concealing for some time his authorship of the *Essay on Man*.³ Drawing room and coffee-house buzzed with speculation as to the identity of the new poet who had arisen to challenge the poetic primacy of Mr. Pope. Mystification was always dear to Pope in and by itself; but there were many enemies who might, he feared, attack him on the score of religious orthodoxy. Could they, by the stratagem of anonymity be trapped into praise which could not afterwards be withdrawn?⁴ Pope writes to Caryll on March 8, 1733, that "I find there is a sort of faction to set up the author and his piece in opposition to me."

In November, 1733, appeared anonymously Pope's "versification" of Donne's second satire, and on January 16, 1734, with the author's name, the *Moral Essay*, "Of the Characters of Men"; a week later (January 24) came out the fourth epistle of the *Essay on Man*. The four epistles were then published together in a single volume on May 2, still without Pope's name, but with virtual abandonment of anonymity by the presence of the name of Boling-broke as their patron. On July 4 appeared the "Second Satire of the Second Book of Horace," *To Mr. Bethel* and in December, *Sober Advice from Horace*.[5] On January 2, 1735 there flashed out upon the fogs of a London winter Pope's most brilliant achievement in Horatian satire, and one of the lasting monuments of his genius, the *Epistle to Dr. Arbuthnot*, to be followed a month later by the last of the *Moral Essays*, "Of the Characters of Women."

I have gone thus minutely into the literary chro-nology of these two years, because I wish to make plain that the *Essay on Man*, the Satires, and the *Moral Essays*, which are a blending of the didactic and the satirical, are the product of a single, or at least a simultaneous, literary inspiration—a fact which is obscured by the arrangement into separate categories in collected editions of the poet's works. They are all ethical writings "in the Horatian way." In all of them Pope has "stooped to truth" and abandoned the maze of fancy and the "false mirror" of what he calls wit, or what we should call inventive fiction. Had Pope died in the spring of 1735, his literary reputation would have been essentially what it actually is. The poet who in 1717 seemed on the way to become a romantic poet, the poet of fancy and pathos, the elegiac singer of Eloisa in her gloomy cloister of the Paraclete, or of the Unfortunate Lady, that beckoning ghost along the moon-light shade, her bleeding bosom transfixed with visionary sword, has turned from "sounds to things," and in the everyday world of commonplace reality has moralized his song, and written didactic poetry.

The word "didactic" is today a word of very ill repute; nor is the word "moralize" in any better odour. If out of favour everywhere, these words are particularly repugnant to most present-day theories of poetry. Modern critics would, I suppose, be willing that we should learn from literature in the sense that we enlarge the scope of our imaginative experience and sharpen our perception of beauty; but anything like a definite precept or a moral is supposed to be utterly at variance with the idea of art, and Croce's doctrine of intuition seems to outlaw from the realm of poetry any formulation of truth arrived at by the process of rational thought.

Whether this limitation of the field of art be true or false, it is well to remember that it is entirely a pro-hibition of modern times. To any poet or critic earlier than the nineteenth century, it would have seemed a preposterous notion that poetry may not teach as well as please. Horace in the *Ars Poetica* leaves no doubt of his opinion in the matter:

> Aut prodesse volunt aut delectare poetae,
> Aut simul et iucunda et idonea dicere vitae
> . . .   .
> Omne tulit punctum qui miscuit utile dulci,
> Lectorem delectando pariterque monendo. (333-44)

The critics of the Renaissance put their chief em-phasis on the didactic function of poetry. To Sir

Philip Sidney poetry is a more effective teacher than
either philosophy or history. For Vossius, "Poetae
sunt morum doctores."[6] The critical tradition of
seventeenth-century France, the tradition to which
Pope acknowledged allegiance, tended towards a
reversal of the emphasis. For both Racine and
Molière the "great rule of all the rules" is to please.
But for an intelligent reader, it was believed, the
highest pleasure is that which is joined to wisdom. As
Boileau sums up the matter in the *Art Poétique*:

> Qu'en savantes leçons votre muse fertile
> Partout joigne au plaisant le solide et l'utile.
> Un lecteur sage fuit un vain amusement,
> Et veut mettre à profit son divertissement.   (IV, 87-90)

If the great tradition of literary criticism is more
than kindly towards the didactic, the tradition of
poetic practice is to the same effect. If one were to
deny the possibility of producing great poetry with a
consciously didactic purpose, one would have to
relegate to the limbo of inferior art such poems as the
Æneid, the *Divine Comedy*, the *Faery Queene*, and
Paradise Lost. I do not doubt that certain groups of
present-day poets and critics would do so without mis-
giving or regret.

One may grant readily enough, and Pope and his
friends would doubtless have agreed, that the spirit
of partisan propaganda is usually not conducive
to the best art; but this is not the spirit of the best
didactic verse. Every normal human being is in-
terested in questions of right and wrong, of true and

false; and the formulation of a truth, even of a moral truth, is a process not inconsistent with emotional fire. The question to be asked is whether the formulation is essentially poetic—"the impassioned expression which is in the countenance of all science." Has the didactic matter passed through the crucible of poetic genius and come out genuine poetry? If what we read rings true as authentic poetry, it is an unfruitful criticism that would reject it because it is also didactic.

It would be a dull ear, and a duller faculty of imagination, that would not recognize the poetic beauty of such a line as—

> Die of a rose in aromatic pain.

Taken out of its context, it sounds as though it might belong in the purely sensuous art of Keats's *Ode to a Nightingale*:

> Now more than ever seems it rich to die,
> To cease upon the midnight with no pain.

But actually it is part of the poetic development of the thesis that "to possess any of the *sensitive faculties* in a higher degree, would render Man miserable":

> Say what the use, were finer optics giv'n,
> T'inspect a mite, not comprehend the heav'n?
> Or touch, if tremblingly alive all o'er,
> To smart and agonize at ev'ry pore?
> Or, quick effluvia darting thro' the brain,
> Die of a rose in aromatic pain?
> If nature thunder'd in his op'ning ears,
> And stunn'd him with the music of the spheres,
> How would he wish that Heav'n had left him still
> The whisp'ring Zephyr, and the purling rill? (I, 195-204)

The phrase "to possess any of the *sensitive faculties* in a higher degree, would render Man miserable" is as unmistakably prose as Pope's development of it is clearly poetry.

Similarly it is in the development of the thesis that "throughout the whole visible world, an universal *order* and gradation in the sensual and mental faculties is observed" that Pope produced the supreme artistry of—

> The spider's touch how exquisitely fine!
> Feels at each thread, and lives along the line.   (217-18)

lines with fineness of touch as exquisite as that which they describe, and lines packed with poetry.

The specifically didactic poem, such as the *Essay on Man*, does not merely suggest instruction; it begins, as we have seen, with an abstract proposition, a philosophical thesis. It is in its inception a poetry of intellectual ideas rather than of sensations and emotions. Such is the raw material thrown into the crucible of poetic creation. In the poetry which emerges the intellectual idea is still present, but it is now transfigured: what was a thesis has become an image; the abstract has taken on concretion; what was dead and inert now glows incandescent with poetic fire; what was somewhat baldly prose has taken on the rhythm and texture of an exquisitely modulated verse.

The didactic poem, when it is really poetry, uses its logical argument chiefly as the structural framework which shall give to it coherence and a larger unity. A sonnet of Wordsworth may build its poetry on an abstract intellectual conception; but this conception will be a single idea, and the restricted compass of fourteen lines neither permits nor requires an argument. Even in the sonnet-sequence the logical development is usually not formal enough to achieve the cumulative effect, the artistic momentum, of a longer poem. The sequence remains a series of short poetic flights. In the didactic poem the formal argument has the same function as the mere story of the narrative poem. Plot and character and situation do not make a poem. If we want a story for the story's own sake, we had much better look for it in prose. In a narrative *poem* the story is but the raw material, the occasion, for the imagery and the music, the play of contrasting ideas, and the poignant poetic phrase. We surely do not value *Paradise Lost* chiefly on the score of its fable. Nor does the *Essay on Man* stand or fall with the consistency of its philosophical argument.

It would be idle to pretend that this transformation has taken place in every line, or in every paragraph of the *Essay on Man*. Between the passages which glow with indubitable poetry there intervene others which retain more of their original character of philosophical abstraction and of the argumentative, passages which are poetry only in virtue of the competence of their metrical form and the terse vigour of their phrasing. Pope and the critics of his school were thoroughly aware that didactic poetry is by its nature of a lower order than the epic or the tragic or the greater ode, of an order less removed than these from the cool regions of prose. Pope had *stooped* to Truth when he moralized

his song. The poem is called an "essay"; its books are
"epistles." In a note "To the Reader" prefixed to the
first edition of the first epistle, the publisher wrote:

> As the Epistolary Way of Writing hath prevailed
> much of late, we have ventured to publish this Piece
> composed some Time since, and whose Author chose
> this Manner, notwithstanding his Subject was high
> and of dignity, because of its being mixt with *Argu-
> ment*, which of its Nature approacheth to Prose.

And in "The Design," prefixed to the edition of 1735,
the author, no longer anonymous, says:

> I was unable to treat this part of my subject more
> in *detail* without becoming dry and tedious; or more
> *poetically*, without sacrificing perspicuity to orna-
> ment.

He has "proposed to write some pieces on Human
Life and Manners, such as (to use my lord Bacon's
expression) *come home to Men's Business and Bosoms*."
It is in the same tone that the poem itself opens.
The poet and his philosopher-friend are to "expatiate free o'er all this scene of Man" (where
expatiate has its literal meaning of "walk about, roam
at will"); like sportsmen, they are to "*beat* this ample
field"; "*shoot* Folly as it flies, and *catch* the Manners
living as they rise." This metaphor of the hunting
field seemed to Warton "much below the dignity of
the subject, and an unnatural mixture of the ludicrous and serious";[7] but it is precisely this blending of
serious matter with the familiar, easy-going manner
of the "epistolary way of writing" that Pope chose as
the temper of his poem, a temper which was to find
room for occasional touches of good-natured satire—

"Laugh where we must"—and yet to "vindicate the ways of God to Man." Pope has ended his exordium with a deliberate echo of the line which closes the first paragraph of *Paradise Lost*; but the two passages are poles asunder. Pope has deliberately chosen that "middle flight" which Milton proudly rejects.

If, then, we would read the *Essay on Man* with the same spirit that its author writ, we must never forget that he has undertaken to treat poetically of a subject "high and of dignity" in the familiar epistolary manner. In the concluding paragraph of the fourth epistle he reiterates this idea. It has been his aim—

> happily to steer
> From grave to gay, from lively to severe:
> Correct with spirit, eloquent with ease,
> Intent to reason, or polite to please.   (379-82)

Pope will speak to us as the cultivated gentleman, "polite to please," talking freely with his friend, moved at times to an impassioned eloquence by the import of his theme, dropping back again into matter-of-fact utterance, now flashing into witty epigram, now giving free rein to playful fancy. He never assumes the rôle of the rhapsodic prophet, who has, like Milton, prayed that his lips might be touched and purified with the hallowed fire of the altar. For Milton poetry is a sacramental mystery; for Pope it is an exacting social art.

II

If Pope is not an inspired prophet, neither is he in any adequate sense of the word a philosopher. Bishop

Warburton, in so many ways the evil genius of Pope's later years and of his literary reputation after his death, in his heavy-footed commentary on the poem has, with great ingenuity but little taste or judgment, distorted it into a systematic "philosophical inquiry" of impeccable orthodoxy. What Pope had called an "essay," a tentative sketch, Warburton tried to erect into a treatise. For the strict rigours of logical thought Pope was wholly unfitted, both by the native character of his mind and by the haphazard course of his very meagre schooling. For the subtle distinctions of metaphysics he and the whole circle of the Queen Anne wits had a sublime contempt. Were not the metaphysicians sworn enemies of good sense, and so high among the Dunces? Pope had some first-hand acquaintance with Locke, whom as a champion of good sense he heartily admired; but most of his philosophical tenets had been absorbed from Bolingbroke, his "guide, philosopher, and friend," who, if not merely an amateur, was not more than an accomplished dilettante in philosophy, critical and eclectic rather than systematic and profound. That the fundamental optimism of Bolingbroke which informs also the *Essay on Man* was derived in large measure from the *Théodicée* of Leibnitz, Pope seems not to have known until after his poem had been published in its entirety.

It had been Pope's intention to exclude from "a strictly philosophical subject" any direct mention of Christian doctrine,[8] just as many centuries before him the theologian Boethius had rigorously restricted his

De Consolatione to the consolations of pagan philosophy. But he had no wish to write in opposition to the Christian faith; and he does not seem to have been aware, till the Swiss theologian M. Crousaz pointed it out in his captious and clumsy *Examen*, published in 1737, that the "natural religion" which he had imbibed from Bolingbroke was deistic in its tendency, and in more than one particular definitely incompatible with Christian revelation, that, to borrow a sonorous phrase from Dr. Johnson, it "represented the whole course of things as a necessary concatenation of indissoluble fatality." Pope had no wish to be numbered among the deists; and he welcomed to his bosom his stout vindicator Warburton, who in a series of letters published in 1738, later put together as the "Commentary," proved him to be the most orthodox of Christians. His letter of thanks to Warburton, dated April 11, 1739, is a curious document:

> You have made my system as clear as I ought to have done, and could not. It is indeed the same system as mine, but illustrated with a ray of your own, as they say our natural body is the same still when it is glorified. I am sure I like it better than I did before, and so will every man else. I know I meant just what you explain; but I did not explain my own meaning as well as you. You understand me as well as I do myself; but you express me better than I could express myself.

Pope is, indeed, no systematic philosopher; and it is easy enough to convict the *Essay on Man* of inconsistencies and of downright contradictions, if one subjects it to the same sort of strict logical scrutiny that one would give to a treatise by a professed philosopher. The *Essay* is open also to the charge which Johnson brought against it, that it tells us only what any man of moderate intelligence already knows, that without "the dazzling splendour of imagery and the seductive powers of eloquence" it is nothing. "Surely a man of no very comprehensive search may venture to say that he has heard all this before; but it was never till now recommended by such a blaze of embellishment, or such sweetness of melody." But if the philosophy is commonplace, what every intelligent reader was expected to know, it is but the more suitable as the material of poetry written in conformity with Pope's theory of poetic art:

> What oft was thought, but ne'er so well express'd;
> Something, whose truth convinc'd at sight we find,
> That gives us back the image of our mind.

Because it was neither new nor very profound, it thrilled the England of 1733 as Tennyson's *In Memoriam* thrilled the England and America of 1850. Of the two poems the *Essay* has stood the wear of time at least as well as its Victorian counterpart.

Pope was not a philosopher, but he was a poet. If he failed to grasp the logical implications of the various theses which he took over from Bolingbroke, he was keenly alive to their imaginative values, their power to touch the reader's heart. We shall do well, then, to concern ourselves only secondarily with the philosophical import of the *Essay on Man*, and to devote first attention to an analysis of it as poetry.

The argument of Epistle I declares that it is to treat "of the Nature and State of Man with respect to the Universe." This is forbiddingly philosophical and completely prosaic. In a very different manner is Pope's poetical summary of Epistle I as resumed in the opening lines of the second epistle. There man's "state with respect to the universe" is presented not to the logical faculty but to the imagination:

> Plac'd on this isthmus of a middle state,
> A Being darkly wise, and rudely great:
> . . .   . . .
> In doubt his Mind or Body to prefer;
> Born but to die, and reas'ning but to err;
> . . .   .
> Created half to rise, and half to fall;
> Great lord of all things, yet a prey to all;
> Sole judge of Truth, in endless Error hurl'd;
> The glory, jest, and riddle of the world!   (II, 3-18)

This is the theme which, with its variations, inspires the whole of Epistle I—the paradox of man, his greatness and appalling insignificance; a little higher than the beasts, a little lower than the angels; amazing both in his knowledge and in his ignorance—a theme that teases us out of thought, and one instinct with deep emotion. It is on this theme that Hamlet also meditates, on man so noble in reason, so infinite in faculty, in form and moving so express and admirable, and yet only the quintessence of dust, the goodly frame of the earth below his feet but a sterile promontory jutting into the infinite sea, the sky above him fretted with golden fire and yet no other thing than a foul and pestilent congregation of vapours. Hamlet,

like Pope, one may remark, is nine parts poet and wit
and only one part philosopher.

In its final form, Epistle I consists of 294 lines. It
is divided into ten numbered sections. Each of these
sections has a poetic unity of its own; the sequence
of them, as they develop the argument, builds up into
the greater unity of the whole epistle. The first three
of these sections develop the theme of the limitation
of man's knowledge. We can reason but from what
we know; of man we can "see but his station here," of
God we can trace only his manifestations in our own
world. Only—

> He, who thro' vast immensity can pierce,
> See worlds on worlds compose one universe
> . . .   .
> May tell why Heav'n has made us as we are. (I, 23-8)

Such comprehensive vision belongs only to God; it is
presumptuous for man even to ask why he is "form'd
so weak, so little, why so blind"—

> His time a moment, and a point his space.   (I, 72)

He must recognize humbly that God, who sees the
whole, has given us that measure of knowledge which
his wisdom deems best for us. So far we are taken by
Sections i and ii. With Section iii, the theme of limited
knowledge takes on a greater intensity of emotion and
a corresponding wealth of imagery. Our happiness
depends on our ignorance of the future; for ignorance
is the only soil from which may spring our great con-
soler hope. It will be worth our while to observe in
some detail the way in which this abstract proposi-

tion is transmuted into deeply moving poetry. The opening couplet of the section reads:

> Heav'n from all creatures hides the book of Fate,
> All but the page prescrib'd, their present state.   (I, 77-8)

We are like school-children, conning day by day the page prescribed for our lesson. We may by memory review the pages which have gone before; we may by our reason make some uncertain guess at the pages which immediately follow; but the divine school-master holds down with his finger all the pages which lie ahead, not even revealing whether they are to be many or few. He hides—

> From brutes what men, from men what spirits know;
> Or who could suffer Being here below?   (I, 79-80)

Then for a moment we are shown the lamb whose reason is so restricted that he is mercifully blind to his impending slaughter—

> Pleas'd to the last he crops the flow'ry food,
> And licks the hand just rais'd to shed his blood. (I, 83-4)

For us, no less than the lamb, this blindness to the future is a kindly gift of heaven. As the lamb is mercifully ignorant that he is to be sacrificed to a higher good, so we by our ignorance are able to "fill the circle marked" for us by a God impartially concerned that every creature shall subserve his proper end—

> Who sees with equal eye, as God of all,
> A hero perish, or a sparrow fall,
> Atoms or systems into ruin hurl'd,
> And now a bubble burst, and now a world. (I, 87-90)

Man's proper attitude is one of humility and hope:

> Hope humbly then; with trembling pinions soar;
> Wait the great teacher Death; and God adore.   (I, 91-2)

The figure of the schoolmaster is resumed, though with a variation. It is death that is to turn the last page of our mortal textbook and open for us an immortal volume, the hope of which is to be our blessing now.

> Hope springs eternal in the human breast;
> Man never Is, but always To be blest:
> The soul, uneasy and confin'd from home,
> Rests and expatiates in a life to come.   (I, 95-8)

Then follow fourteen lines—just the measure of a sonnet—so exquisite in their music, so moving in their tenderness, that they have found lodgement in every memory, which enforce the hope of immortality by an appeal to the poor Indian to whose "untutor'd mind" simple Nature has given the hope of a humble heaven, where "his faithful dog shall bear him company."

Sections iv and v are more argumentative and less impassioned. With the humility of the poor Indian, the child of instinct, who "asks no angel's wing, no seraph's fire" is contrasted the man of proud reason who, weighing his opinion against Providence, presumes to find fault with the state which God has ordained for man,

> Rejudge his justice, be the GOD of GOD,

who, assuming that the universe was made for his pleasure—

> Seas roll to waft me, suns to light me rise;
> My foot-stool earth, my canopy the skies! (I, 140-1)

cries out because God has permitted storms and earthquakes and, worst of all, the existence of moral evil.

Sections vi-ix return to the theme of limitation, the limitation now not of man's knowledge, but of his powers and faculties. In the third book of the *Essay concerning Human Understanding* (vi, 12), Locke introduces, by way of digression, the Neo-Platonic doctrine of the Great Chain of Being, which was to become chief cornerstone of eighteenth-century optimism:[9]

> It is not impossible to conceive, nor repugnant to reason, that there may be many species of spirits, as much separated and diversified one from another by distinct properties whereof we have no ideas, as the species of sensible things are distinguished one from another by qualities which we know and observe in them. That there should be more species of intelligent creatures above us, than there are of sensible and material below us, is probable to me from hence: that in all the visible corporeal world, we see no chasms or gaps. All quite down from us the descent is by easy steps, and a continued series of things, that in each remove differ very little one from the other. . . . And when we consider the infinite power and wisdom of the Maker, we have reason to think that it is suitable to the magnificent harmony of the universe, and the great design and infinite goodness of the Architect, that the species of creatures should also, by gentle degrees, ascend upward from us toward his infinite perfection, as we see they gradually descend from us downwards.

Locke develops this idea through a page and a half of his essay. The conception of a graduated "scale

of being," "from Infinite to thee, from thee to nothing" is one which, whatever its philosophical defects,
cannot but make a powerful appeal to the imagination. Addison whose ambition it was to bring "Philosophy out of Closets and Libraries, Schools and
Colleges, to dwell in Clubs and Assemblies, at Tea-
Tables and in Coffee-Houses," seized upon it as the
theme of No. 519 of the *Spectator*, with proper acknowledgment to Locke. It may well have been in
the *Spectator* that the idea first came to Pope's attention. But it could have come to him from many
sources. Thomson had used it in his *Seasons* (*Summer*
333-6):

> Has any seen
> The mighty chain of beings, lessening down
> From infinite perfection to the brink
> Of dreary nothing, desolate abyss!

Thomson used the idea, as does Pope, to show the
impious presumption of those who "tax Creative Wisdom." It is the central idea of the third chapter of
Archbishop King's *Essay on the Origin of Evil*, published in 1731 in an English translation with copious
notes by Edmund Law—a book with which Pope
seems certainly to have been acquainted. The idea is
alluded to at some length in No. 49 of Bolingbroke's
Fragments, and may well have been elaborated in
Bolingbroke's conversations with Pope.

In the sober sentences of John Locke there is already present a strong imaginative appeal; and this
appeal had given to the concept a currency which
greatly exceeded the bounds of closet and library,

schools and colleges, and had established it at tea-tables and in coffee-houses. It was material ideally suited to the genius of Mr. Pope, which stooping to truth, can yet give to that truth a poetic ardour whose fire has none of the obscuring smoke that so often wreathes the higher flights of poesy:

> See, thro' this air, this ocean, and this earth,
> All matter quick, and bursting into birth.
> Above, how high, progressive life may go!
> Around, how wide! how deep extend below!
> Vast chain of Being! which from God began,
> Natures æthereal, human, angel, man,
> Beast, bird, fish, insect, what no eye can see,
> No glass can reach; from Infinite to thee,
> From thee to Nothing.   (I, 233-41)

From these lines we turn the page and find another passage of indubitable poetry, and one which again reaches just the measure of a sonnet, a passage which crowds into fourteen lines (i, 267-80) the pantheistic theology which was a century later to receive poetic expression from Wordsworth, from Byron, and from Shelley. Such didactic verse as this needs no apology. It is matter of the intellect, informed with the *vis vivida* of impassioned poetry.

From the eloquence of these lines we pass on to the famous conclusion of the epistle, again just fourteen lines in length, of which the sestet reads:

> All Nature is but Art, unknown to thee;
> All Chance, Direction, which thou canst not see;
> All Discord, Harmony not understood;
> All partial Evil, universal Good:
> And spite of Pride, in erring Reason's spite,
> One truth is clear, WHATEVER IS, IS RIGHT.

This suggestion of the sonnet furnishes, I think, the hint as to the way in which the modern reader can best read the *Essay on Man*. Its more or less deistic philosophy was respectable enough in its day—it was the intellectual currency of Augustan England, accepted at its face value by all but the ultra-orthodox at the one extreme and the completely deistic free-thinkers at the other. For us much of it is hopelessly out of date; some of it is even puerile. We had better leave the philosophy to the historian of eighteenth-century thought. But the poetry of which it is the occasion remains; and it is poetry of a high order.

III

The *Essay on Man* gave, as I have already suggested, to the England of the 1730's the image of its mind,[10] much as *In Memoriam* spoke the thought of 1850. It is interesting to set alongside of the eloquent conclusion of Epistle I of the *Essay* what is probably the most often quoted flight of Tennyson's moralized song:

> Oh yet we trust that somehow good
> Will be the final goal of ill,
> To pangs of nature, sins of will,
> Defects of doubt, and taints of blood;
>
> That nothing walks with aimless feet;
> That not one life shall be destroy'd,
> Or cast as rubbish to the void,
> When God hath made the pile complete;

That not a worm is cloven in vain;
    That not a moth with vain desire
    Is shrivell'd in a fruitless fire,
Or but subserves another's gain.

Behold, we know not anything;
    I can but trust that good shall fall
    At last—far off—at last, to all,
And every winter change to spring. ·

The sixteen lines of Tennyson and the six of Pope give much the same answer to the question which has troubled thoughtful people almost ever since thought began, the question with which a nameless Hebrew poet concerned himself many centuries ago in the Book of Job. How shall one explain the existence of dire evil, moral as well as physical, in a world ordered by an all-powerful, just, and loving God? Both Pope and Tennyson answer that evil is only apparent, that could we see the whole, discord would resolve itself into harmony, partial evil would turn out to be universal good; God is in his heaven, and in his sight all is well with the world. Both speak as optimists, but with a highly significant difference. Pope, in accord with the thought of his generation, is a static optimist; in the best of all possible worlds whatever is *is* right. To Tennyson, imbued with the idea of evolutionary progress, whatever is shall somehow in the end turn to good, "When God hath made the pile complete." To Pope the truth is clear; he speaks with untroubled certitude. Tennyson yearns after his faith and hope, clutching desperately at it, like an infant crying in the night. Though Tennyson's philosophy may be no more satisfactory to our present generation than

Pope's, his manner, that of the groping seeker after truth, is one which we better understand. Pope's clear certainty about all sorts of things is for the modern reader a serious obstacle to the appreciation of his didactic verse. Whence does Pope derive his certitude?

The England of Pope's day had brought to the bar of reason and common sense, and so had settled to its own satisfaction, the great fundamental principles of its life and activity. It is one of the rare periods in the history of thought when all men, or nearly all, are agreed in essentials as to what we ought to do and think, and dispute only as to methods, or as to the corollaries of the main propositions. It is this agreement that one means when one speaks of the "eighteenth-century settlement."

The "glorious Revolution" of 1688 had settled for England the question of political theory. The Stuarts had proclaimed the divine right of kings. The idea is so foreign to our present-day thought that one is in danger of forgetting what it may once have meant to the imagination of a loyal subject. God cares so much for us that he has put our daily affairs, our peace and prosperity, into the hands of a king of his own anointing, who shall speak and act as his immediate deputy. The Puritans had gone further and attempted a theocracy. Cromwell was but "Lord Protector"; God himself was king and president, his word the highest law, his throne the last tribunal. But such notions as these could have no place in a generation of enlightenment and good sense. The new dream, not quite so splendid, but no less a triumph of faith over experience, the dream of democracy, still lay ahead. Before the eighteenth century was ended the crusading armies of the French Republic were proclaiming to all Europe the gospel of Liberty, Equality, Fraternity: that we are all brothers, and each his brother's keeper; that out of the collective unwisdom of the many there shall come forth a corporate wisdom. The "laws of Nature and of Nature's God" have so ordained it. *Vox populi vox dei*—the divine right not of a king but of a majority. These ideas were to set on fire the imagination of a youthful Wordsworth, a Shelley, a Tennyson. Pope and his generation had to be content with the ideal of a vaguely defined "social contract," founded on the greatest good of the greatest number, seeking its sanction not in the will of God, nor in the inalienable "rights of man," but in cool reason and common sense. In actual practice the government of Great Britain was a selfish oligarchy of the upper and middle classes; and the first two Hanoverians did not wear the royal robes in such fashion as to stimulate any warmth of loyalty. Patriotism was an outmoded sentiment; one chose rather to be a "citizen of the world."

Nor was there anything in the moral order to enlist men's higher loyalties. Pope's age was done with the austere idealism of the Puritans, and with the light-hearted license which, in fashionable circles at least, had been the vogue between 1660 and 1688. Swift and Addison and Pope are contemptuous both of "enthusiast" and of libertine or fop. Either offends in equal measure against that decent mean which is good sense, good taste, and therefore good morality. The way of the transgressor may often prove hard; but no less hard is the way of the devoted martyr. One should be content to be that "noblest work of God," an honest man.

Like politics and morals, religion also was brought into harmony with reason and good sense. Though Pope and most of his friends were professing Christians—Swift and Parnell were priests of the established Church, and Atterbury a lord bishop—there was little fervour in the faith of any of them. Except in the heat of controversy, it is not easy to distinguish between the religion of an orthodox divine such as Swift and the free-thinking deists whom he despised. The creed of deism, or "natural" religion, was that to which, so men thought, one is inevitably driven by innate human reason; its articles—a God who is seen in nature, and is nature's great "first cause"; charity and justice as the most acceptable worship; a future life of rewards and punishments—are those which are common to all respectable religions the world over, including that of Pope's "poor Indian." Christian revelation constitutes, no doubt, a desirable supplement to natural religion, but one will emphasize its reasonableness rather than its supernatural character. And so religion becomes for nearly everyone save William Law[11] an impersonal affair, whose chief concern is decent living. There is a wide difference between the temper of Pope's *Universal Prayer* and Newman's "Lead Kindly Light"—or between Addison's "Spacious Firmament on High" and the hymns of the "enthusiast" Charles Wesley. Nor does natural religion meditate often on the awful mysteries of life and death.

Love of country or of humanity at large, the passion for the right, the great mysteries of religion— these are the wellsprings of our greater loyalties; for Pope and his generation these springs have run nearly dry. The "eighteenth-century settlement," with its bland disregard of what cannot be readily rationalized, with its complacent assurance of complete certainty, imposed upon the moralized song of Pope rather serious limitations. The theme of man's "middle state," his paradoxical blending of weakness and strength, which is developed in the first epistle of the *Essay on Man*, is for Pope, and so for Pope's reader, fraught with true poetic fire. In the other three epistles, which deal with man "as an individual," the conflict of reason and self-love and the balance of virtue and vice, with the social order, with the problem of happiness, there is too often a sense of chill sterility, broken to be sure by such fine passages as that in Epistle III which sings the instinctive wisdom of the lower animals:

> Who made the spider parallels design,
> Sure as Demoivre, without rule or line?
> Who did the stork, Columbus-like, explore
> Heav'ns not his own, and worlds unknown before?
> Who calls the council, states the certain day,
> Who forms the phalanx, and who points the way?

or again: (III, 103-8)

> Learn of the little Nautilus to sail,
> Spread the thin oar, and catch the driving gale. (III, 177-8)

The reader of the fourth epistle, least poetic of the four, is rewarded by such a line as—

> The soul's calm sun-shine, and the heart-felt joy,
>
> (IV, 168)

besides many a line which gives the intellectual pleasure of terse, compact epigram.

But in Epistles II, III, and IV there are too many passages of merely versified argumentation—however competent the versification may be; and the argumentation is too frequently faulty argument. Not even the dialectic ingenuities of a Warburton can give consistency to the varying ideas which Pope had picked up here and there. Man is for the purposes of one argument regarded as free to shape his own destiny, for the purposes of another as the helpless victim of his "ruling passion"—or, as we should phrase it today, of a psychological determinism. At one time Pope assumes with Shaftesbury the essential goodness and benevolence of the natural man; at another he echoes Mandeville's famous paradox that private vices make for public benefits.

The ethical epistles, which since Warburton's edition of 1751 have gone under the title of *Moral Essays*, are prevailingly pitched lower than the epistles of the *Essay on Man*. There is less of philosophical argument, more of concrete illustration; and the illustrations are in large part satiric in character. These epistles, indeed, occupy middle ground between the didactic and the satiric. In the collected "Works" of 1735, the *Epistle to Dr. Arbuthnot*, later used as Prologue to the Satires, is associated with these epistles rather than with the First and Second Satires of the Second Book of Horace. The *Epistle to Cobham*, "Of the Knowledge and Characters of Men," deals only light-heartedly with the springs of human action and the fashionable doctrine of the "ruling passion" which is "strong in death." It is at its best in the satirical "character" of the Duke of Wharton, and in the witty death-bed scenes with which it closes. The much more brilliant "Of the Characters of Women" is chiefly memorable as a portrait-gallery of female foibles and inconstancies—Narcissa, Flavia, Chloe, and the great Atossa. The *Epistle to Lord Bathurst* "Of the Use of Riches," is in the same temper as the Horatian satires on the misuse of wealth, and only less telling than *Seventeen Hundred and Thirty Eight*, which was to become the "Epilogue to the Satires." When one thinks of the *Epistle to the Earl of Burlington*, it is the satiric picture of Timon's villa, rather than the didactic thesis that utility and good sense are the indispensable foundation of good taste, that at once springs to the memory.

On such themes as those treated in the *Moral Essays*, Pope has much to say that is witty and entertaining, his satire hits the mark; but the clear certainties of the "eighteenth-century settlement" do not make for much profundity of thought or poignancy of feeling. One need not regret that Pope never brought to completion his grandiose plan of "completing my ethic work in four books," of which the *Essay on Man* would have constituted Book I, and which was to include an "Essay on Education," and a discussion of "Government, both ecclesiastical and civil" and of "Morality, in eight or nine of the most concerning branches of it."[12] A comprehensive ethical system such as this would have demanded a more orderly and better disciplined mind than that of Pope. But we can be very glad indeed that we have the poetic badinage of the *Moral Essays*, and the graver poetry of the first epistle of the *Essay on Man*. This first epistle is the triumphant proof, if proof is needed, that didactic poetry is not a contradiction in terms.

When Bolingbroke urged Pope to moralize his song, he made a sound literary appraisal of his friend's genius. "Universal as his talents are, this is eminently and peculiarly his, above all the writers I know, living or dead." Had the promise of 1717, of *Eloisa* and the *Unfortunate Lady*, been fulfilled, Pope might conceivably have become a more fastidious and less volcanic Byron. Instead, he turned, after Homer was all translated, to satire and the didactic poem; stooping to truth, he moralized his song.

In the *Epistle to Dr. Arbuthnot*, and in the first epistle of the *Essay on Man*, he produced poetic masterpieces which in their kind have not been equalled, nor approached, by any English poet since his day. If the kind is not, as Pope clearly recognized, one of the more exalted poetic orders, it is probably the kind in which it is hardest to achieve an artistic masterpiece. That was, at any rate, the opinion of Pope's ardent vindicator, Lord Byron. In the course of his controversy with Rev. W. L. Bowles, Byron wrote:

> In my mind, the highest of all poetry is ethical poetry . . . It requires more mind, more wisdom, more power, than all the "forests" that were ever "walked for their description," and all the epics that ever were founded upon fields of battle . . . It is the fashion of the day to lay great stress upon what they call "imagination" and "invention," the two commonest of qualities: an Irish peasant with a little whisky in his head will imagine and invent more than would furnish forth a modern poem.[13]

I think we have all read some more recent poems whose inspiration suggests Byron's "peasant with a little whisky in his head." From them we may be glad to turn back to the *mind*, and *wisdom*, and *power* which inform the ethical poetry of Alexander Pope.

VIII

THE ART OF SATIRE

I

IN THE *Epistle to the Earl of Burlington*, which we now know as the fourth *Moral Essay*, "Of the Use of Riches," which earlier bore the title "Of Taste," Pope invites the reader to pass with him a day at "Timon's villa," "Where all cry out, 'What sums are thrown away!' "—thrown away on a tasteless display of vulgar magnificence,

> So proud, so grand; of that stupendous air,
> Soft and Agreeable come never there.   (101-2)

Both the Brobdingnagian house and the grounds, laboured with hot terrace on hot terrace, with the balanced formality of geometrical gardening, with the "inverted Nature" of topiary shrubbery, seem but "huge heaps of littleness." There is a library whose shelves display all the books which a gentleman should own, but need not read. There is a luxuriously furnished and elaborately decorated private chapel, whose silver bell "summons you to all the Pride of Pray'r," whose soft-spoken ministrant "never mentions Hell to ears polite." In the great marble dining hall most sumptuous viands are ceremoniously set before you; but over-numerous, over-zealous serving men snatch the plate away before you have more than tasted, so that you leave the table, "in plenty starving, tantaliz'd in State."

The Epistle was published on December 14, 1731, and immediately Pope found himself the target of very unpleasant attacks. Contemporary readers identified Timon's villa with Cannons, country seat of the Duke of Chandos, a nobleman who had, so they said, been one of Pope's most generous patrons. How far they were right in this identification, which Pope indignantly denied and zealously sought to refute, one cannot say with certainty.[1] For the appraisal of the poet's personal character the question is of some consequence; for the delighted reader of his brilliant satire the answer makes little difference. The Duke of Chandos is for us a quite forgotten personage, a "puny insect" whose wings have lost all the tinsel of former grandeur; but "Timon" has taken permanent place alongside of the Trimalchio of Petronius as a perpetual type of the lavish vulgarity of tasteless opulence. We recognize him across the gap of two centuries, and chuckle, with a touch of malice, as we identify some living successor, at whose newly-rich table we have been "tantaliz'd in State." Such malicious glee of recognition is of the very essence of great satire. Pope has caught and pilloried for us something typical and permanent, something which both disgusts and amuses.

Satire is the artistic refinement of a primitive instinct, still very much alive in most of us, the instinct to laugh at what we hate. The insensitive boor makes merry over physical deformity—as poor crippled Mr. Pope could abundantly testify; the schoolboy calls names—in accordance with his own artistic canons; the mob jeers; and so long as there is present both ridicule and disapproval, we have at least the raw material of satire. Satire is the fine art of calling names. It is the literary expression of a laughter which implies rebuke, a laughter spiced with something of malice, a scornful amusement at the follies and foibles of an individual or of human nature and human institutions in general.

It is essential that both these elements be present. If there is no implication of rebuke, we have merely good-natured raillery and humour. We smile at the foibles of the charmingly empty-headed Belinda, but with no breath of disapproval—

> If to her share some female errors fall,
> Look on her face, and you'll forget 'em all.

A stern moralist could find much to say in rebuke of Falstaff. Is he not liar, thief, and glutton—a most unedifying example of elderly debauchery, "a villainous abominable misleader of youth." But Shakespeare does not hold him up for censure; and Shakespeare's audience forgets all its moral standards, and laughs whole-heartedly at, and with, this incomparable figure of purely comic humour, as three generations of readers have laughed at the hope which springs eternal in the sanguine breast of Mr. Micawber, with never a thought of rebuke for his irresponsible shiftlessness. If, on the other hand, the element of ridicule is lacking, the rebuke becomes mere accusation and invective. Between these two extremes—the outer confines of the comic and the frontiers of sheer invective—lies the region of satire. Sometimes, as with

Chaucer, with Addison, or with Pope in the *Rape of the Lock*, it hovers just outside the gates of comedy; with Swift and with Juvenal, when their indignation is most savage, it verges on the very limits of invective.

Satire is peculiarly one of the arts of civilization; for it presupposes a body of settled social standards which shall serve as sanction for its rebuke, and at the same time a certain security and resultant tolerance in the application of the standards. When this assurance is lacking, offenders against accepted convention are usually punished with something grimmer than a lampoon. One must be able to afford the tolerance even of bitter laughter. If it is essentially a civilized art, it seems also to belong especially to Latin civilization. There is no trace of it in the Bible, unless perhaps for a passing flicker once or twice in the Book of Job; there is hardly more of it in the primitive literature of the Germanic north, unless one should dignify by the name of satire the boastful jeers of a Beowulfian "flyting." And it is more a product of Roman literature than of Greek—though one is not likely to forget either Aristophanes or Lucian; but Lucian, at any rate, was a Romanized Greek, and the critics tell us that his prose style is coloured with Latinisms. It is significant that the word *satire* is a Latin word, while most of our literary labels—drama, epic, lyric, ode—are Greek.

Satire as a distinct literary form came into full flower in Augustan Rome with Horace and Persius and Juvenal, the period when Roman civilization was at its finest. When, after centuries of turbulence and turmoil, Latin Christianity has once more recivilized the western Europe of the later Middle Ages, the satiric temper emerges again in the Goliardic verses attributed to Walter Map, in the *Speculum Stultorum* of Nigellus Wireker, in *Reynard the Fox*, in the *Romance of the Rose*, in our English *Piers Plowman*, and in many a brilliant stroke in the varied pages of Chaucer. Though satire is, perhaps, less a characteristic note of the Renaissance than it is of the more highly disciplined mind of the Middle Ages, we have the extravagant raillery of a Rabelais, and the keen irony of an Erasmus or a Cervantes. Formal satire comes once more into its own in the France of Louis XIV and in the England of Dryden and Pope, when literature and civilization are peculiarly Latinized. During the eighteenth century it continues to flourish, only to recede once more with the oncoming of that profound change in taste and temper which we call the Romantic Movement—that congeries of sentimental humanitarianism, naturalism, primitivism, and wild exoticism which is the complete antithesis of everything Latin. The very temper of satire—that curious balance of discipline and tolerance, of clearly defined standards and a certain geniality in the application of them—is an essentially Latin temper, the temper of the critic rather than of the reformer. The Hebraic temper and the Teutonic give us prophets and reformers; the Latin makes for criticism and satire.

II

But though the mood of satire is far removed from
that of the sentimentally sanguine reformer, the
prophet of some austere Utopia, its criticism is not
always, as with Addison and usually with Horace,
merely that of the dispassionate spectator, genially
amused at our shortcomings. Great satire has behind
it the driving force of moral conviction, a burning
hatred of evil, "the strong antipathy of good to bad."

> When Truth or Virtue an Affront endures,
> Th' Affront is mine, my friend, and should be yours.
> Mine, as a Foe profess'd to false Pretence,
> Who think a Coxcomb's Honour like his Sense;
> Mine, as a Friend to ev'ry worthy mind;
> And mine as Man, who feel for all mankind.
>
> (*Epilogue to the Satires*, II, 199-204)

Though Pope's "strong antipathies" were, no doubt,
sometimes animated by personal resentment and
wounded pride, I see no reason for doubting the sincerity of his indignation at the affronts endured by
"truth or virtue," or of his belief that his satire was a
"sacred weapon, left for truth's defence"—

> Rev'rent I touch thee! but with honest zeal,
> To rouse the Watchmen of the public Weal.
>
> (*Epilogue to the Satires*, II, 216-17)

Even the hatred engendered from personal resentment is, if not a noble passion, none the less a very
intense passion; and intensity is one of the elements
of great literature. There is a certain sublimity in personal hatred when the hatred is sufficiently intense.

Pope's satire, even when actuated solely by indignation at public wrong, stops short of the devastating bitterness, the *sæva indignatio*, aroused in the soul of Swift by the evil and corruption which he saw in all the social relations of mankind. One contemplates the loathsome Yahoos and their bestial nastiness, or one sees through the burning eyes of Juvenal the senseless luxury and incredible vice of imperial Rome, with disgust and horror rather than with even a scornful laughter. This is not in the spirit of the critic, nor even of the reformer; it is such an accusation as Satan himself might deliver at the great assize. It seems to seek not castigation but annihilation, as Lear, raging on the heath, bids the furious elements—

> Smite flat the thick, rotundity of the world,
> Crack nature's moulds, all germins spill at once
> That make ingrateful man.

But, as Edward Young says in the Preface to *Love of Fame: the Universal Passion* (1725-6), "laughing satire bids the fairest for success"; and the prevailing tone of Pope's satire is like that of Dryden, comic rather than tragic; it is in the mood not of Satan but of Mephistopheles, a mood of scornful amusement at human frailties and foibles, at knavery and folly. But even "laughing satire" has in it something of the diabolic; for unless there is derision in the laughter, it ceases to be satiric. It is the spirit of mockery rather than of sympathy, the spirit that denies. At the fine spectacle of life it insists on going behind the scenes, where a grimy, sweating stage-hand is pushing on the snow-white swan of Lohengrin. It turns over the glowing tapestry and looks at the loose ends; it prefers the seamy side of things. It looks with the eyes of hate rather than of love, magnifying faults, minimizing virtues. Love may be blind, but hate is a very Argus. It lays bare the hidden fault, and grins at the discovery. It takes the smiling pretences of life, strips off their finery, and looks at life—not naked, but in its underwear.

Satirists sometimes tell us that they write to reform us; it is their most obvious defence against the charge of malice and all uncharitableness. I am doubtful of their complete sincerity in this claim, and even more doubtful whether satire has ever wrought a thorough reformation. The fear of ridicule may lead to the concealment, perhaps even to the repression of knavery and folly; but it can hardly turn the fool to real wisdom. Its function is rather to set the knave and the fool in his true light, to disturb the complacency with which those of us who are not knaves and fools regard the civilization of which we partake, to knock the rose-coloured spectacles from off our social nose. As Boileau finely puts it near the end of his tenth Satire, *A son esprit*, satire is reason's vengeance on the outrages of a fool:

> La satire, en leçons, en nouveautés fertile,
> Sait seule assaisonner le plaisant et l'utile,
> Et, d'un vers qu'elle épure aux rayons du bon sens,
> Détromper les esprits des erreurs de leurs temps.
> Elle seule, bravant l'orgeuil et l'injustice,
> Va jusque sous le dais faire pâlir le vice;
> Et souvent sans rien craindre, à l'aide d'un bon mot,
> Va venger la raison des attentats d'un sot.

Pope's justification of his satire, as set forth in the First Satire of the Second Book of Horace, addressed to Mr. Fortescue, is in similar vein. Fools rush into his head and so he writes. He will "strip the gilding off a knave":

> Yes, while I live, no rich or noble knave,
> Shall walk the world, in credit, to his grave.
> To VIRTUE ONLY AND HER FRIENDS A FRIEND,
> The World beside may murmur, or commend.   (119-22)

Shall the darts of derision be hurled at an individual knave or fool, or at the absurd follies of society in general? Each type of satire has its advantages and its compensating drawbacks. For the contemporary reader who knows the victims, personal satire must always have the greater zest. Pope believed that personal satire was the more effective weapon against general corruption. On August 2, 1734, he wrote in a letter to Dr. Abuthnot:

> General satire in times of general vice has no force and is no punishment: people have ceased to be ashamed of it when so many are joined with them; and it is only by hunting one or two from the herd that any examples can be made. If a man writ all his life against the collective body of the banditti, or against lawyers, would it do the least good, or lessen the body? But if some are hung up or pilloried, it may prevent others. And in my low station, with no other power than this, I hope to deter, if not to reform.

But personal satire, when looked at as literary art, may prove to be very perishable merchandise, and fade with the passing hour. Pope's victims were once well-known figures of London town; one was likely to

run into them at coffee-house or tavern, or to find
oneself opposite them at the dinner table. Now they
are, with few exceptions, merely names preserved, as
Pope himself realized that they would be, like insects
in the clear amber of his art. To recover the personalities, a reader must lose himself in a weary tangle
of footnotes. Personal satire can attain the permanence of great art only when the satirist succeeds
in making the individual stand forth as a type of
universal and unchanging human frailty—and that
requires vision and creative imagination.

Contemporaries saw, or thought they saw, in Pope's
satirical character of "Atossa" the portrait of the
great Sarah, Duchess of Marlborough. Even for us
Sarah Jennings is still a remembered name, sufficiently remembered so that we read the lines with a
malicious pleasure heightened by the identification.
But the character is not merely a success of scandal;
"Atossa" as a creature of poetic imagination has a
universal value. She is the abiding type of a loveless
woman grown old in the domineering caprice of
wealth and power:

> Who, with herself, or others, from her birth
> Finds all her life one warfare upon earth:
> Shines in exposing Knaves, and painting Fools,
> Yet is, whate'er she hates and ridicules.
> No Thought advances, but her Eddy Brain
> Whisks it about, and down it goes again.
> Full sixty years the World has been her Trade,
> The wisest Fool much Time has ever made.
> From loveless youth to unrespected age,
> No Passion gratified except her Rage.
> . . .   .

Her ev'ry turn with Violence pursu'd,
Nor more a storm her Hate than gratitude.

. . .   .

Offend her, and she knows not to forgive;
Oblige her, and she'll hate you while you live.

(*Moral Essays*, II, 117-38)

General satire, though in its nature less perishable than personal, may prove ephemeral with the passing of the particular abuses and follies satirized, unless through these particulars the author has bodied forth the universal and permanent foolishness of the human biped. Social customs are of a day; but foppishness and affectation are always with us. It is the triumph of Swift's satiric art that his Lilliputians have remained for two centuries the perpetual type of human pettiness.

III

Whether general or personal, satire is concerned with the facts of life rather than with romantic fancies. It is an art of heightened realism—at its greatest, of a universalized realism. When it appears, as occasionally it does, in a romantic setting, it shatters at a stroke all romantic glamour. *Candide* and *Don Juan* give us thoroughly disillusioned romance, the romantic trappings are but a foil which heightens the derision. Regions of fancy though they be, both Erewhon and Lilliput are depicted with minute realism of detail. It is interesting to see how Swift has deliberately avoided all the romantic charm which might have gathered about a race of little creatures no bigger than the fairies of *Midsummer Night's Dream*. For the entertainment of Bottom,

Titania's little servitors rob the squirrel's winter
store of nuts, or steal the honey-bag of the humble-
bee. The Lilliputians provide for Gulliver a daily
ration of six beeves, forty sheep, and other victuals,
together with a proportionable quantity of wine and
other liquors; "for the due payment of which his
Majesty gave assignments upon his treasury." They
carefully compute that, since Gulliver's height is
twelve times theirs, his bulk is to theirs as the cube of
twelve, and thus allow him a supply of food sufficient
for 1728 Lilliputians; "by which, the reader may con-
ceive an idea of the ingenuity of that people, as well as
the prudent and exact economy of so great a prince."

The neo-classic formula of Wit and Judgment in
perfect balance is peculiarly applicable to the art of
satire. In this region of literary art "wit" as equivalent to "invention" or "imagination" seems to our
modern preconceptions the proper term. But the wit
must not forget its quality of inventive imagination;
mere cleverness will not serve, nor mere play of
humour. Satiric wit is something rarer and subtler
than humour, something more serious, more intellectual than mere cleverness. Wit points out the
happy choice of a line of attack, finds out the weak
joint in the armour of pretentious folly or triumphant
knavery, and hand in hand with nimble fancy, which
is own cousin to wit, suggests a thousand ingenious
variations on the theme. It is wit of a very high order
that sends Gulliver first to a land of pigmies and
thence to a land of giants, that having laughed at the
pettiness of Lilliput, we may see our own littleness

through the eyes of Brobdingnag; the wit and fancy with which the conception is developed are beyond all praise. The Prince of Lilliput "is taller by almost the breadth of my nail than any of his court, which alone is enough to strike an awe into the beholders." It is wit of a high order that points the rapier with which Pope thrusts and thrusts again at dunce and fop and high-placed knave.

But if great satire needs abundance of fertile wit, there must be present also an equal measure of compensating judgment, which shall give it artistic restraint. It must know not only when and where to strike, but how deep should be the thrust. It is no accident that formal satire, first brought to artistic perfection in Augustan Rome, should have chiefly flourished in periods when the classical tradition has been dominant. John Dryden, great satirist and our first great English critic, in his essay on the *Original and Progress of Satire* insists on the need of that restraint, which his own satiric writing so perfectly exemplifies:

> The nicest and most delicate touches of satire consist in fine raillery. . . . How easy is it to call rogue and villain, and that wittily! But how hard to make a man appear a fool, a blockhead, or knave, without using any of those opprobrious terms! . . . There is still a vast difference betwixt the slovenly butchering of a man, and the fineness of a stroke that separates the head from the body, and leaves it standing in its place. A man may be capable, as Jack Ketch's wife said of his servant, of a plain piece of work, a bare hanging; but to make a malefactor die sweetly was only belonging to her husband.[2]

If one wishes a pattern of "fine raillery," of the perfect balance of satiric wit and restraining judgment, one cannot do better than turn to Dryden's "character" of George Villiers, Duke of Buckingham, in Part I of *Absalom and Achitophel*—

> A man so various that he seem'd to be
> Not one, but all Mankind's Epitome.   (545-6)

"Zimri" is the abiding type of the brilliant but ineffectual versatility of a volatile mind. Dryden thought this portrait his own masterpiece of "fine raillery."

The satirical portrait, or "character," exemplified in Dryden's "Zimri," and in the "Sporus" and "Atticus" of the *Epistle to Dr. Arbuthnot*, is an element that has always bulked large in the tradition of formal satire which derives from Horace. Sometimes it is recognizable as the portrait of a single original, sometimes, as in Young's *Universal Passion*, it is an idealized composite type; but always, to be great, it must have something of the typical, the universal, as the Shadwell of Dryden's *Mac Flecnoe*, "mature in dulness from his tender years," is not merely a more than half-forgotten Restoration playwright and poet laureate, but the type of an almost sublime stupidity and dulness:

> *Shadwell* alone of all my Sons is he
> Who stands confirm'd in full stupidity.
> The rest to some faint meaning make pretence,
> But *Shadwell* never deviates into sense.   (15-18)

The Shadwells are a numerous progeny, even today.

To be completely successful, the satiric portrait must be drawn with at least the appearance of fairness. In this respect Dryden's "Zimri" surpasses his Shadwell. One may exaggerate the faults, but one should not be blind to the victim's virtues. He must seem a victim deserving of your pains; you should not break a mere butterfly on the wheel of artistic satire. And the satirist should at least seem to be writing more in sorrow than in anger. What could surpass the apparent sweetness of temper, the seeming generosity of Mr. Strachey's full-length portrait of Queen Victoria or of the subsidiary portraits which are its corollaries? Here is no cheap railing at everything Victorian; and yet what merciless dissection! The satirist should smile and smile, even when perpetrating his most cunning villainies. If he loses his temper, the fine blade of satire does not cut clean; the weapon becomes a mere bludgeon, and the execution is at best a "slovenly butchering"—the malefactor has not "died sweetly."

This great principle of seeming fair Dryden seldom forgot; but Pope forgets it somewhat frequently. The virulence of his hatred for Lady Mary Wortley Montagu makes of "Sappho" a regrettable caricature; how, one asks, could so disgusting a person ever have been the poet's dear friend? And so with Lord Hervey, Lady Mary's close ally in their assault on Twickenham. The portrait of "Sporus" fails to convince because of the extravagance of its scorn—and that despite the superb energy of its phrasing, its telling images, the sustained power of its verse. There must,

The Poetical Career of Pope

one instinctively feels, be another side to the story—
and any reader of Hervey's *Memoirs* will discover
that he was at least an entertaining annalist. How
could such "florid impotence" and shallow emptiness
have aroused such vitriolic hatred? Why should
"this bug with gilded wings, this painted child of dirt,
that stinks and stings" have called forth such devastating energy of satire?

But if Pope in the portrait of "Sporus" allowed
wit to outrun restraining judgment, he has in his
character of "Atticus" achieved a well-nigh perfect
masterpiece. Just what may have been the provocation which called it forth is one of the tangled problems in Pope's biography. Pope and Addison had been
for a time on terms of friendly intercourse, though
between natures so diverse no great intimacy of
friendship is readily conceivable. Frost and fire do not
well consort. Pope thought that Addison was jealous
of his literary success and had deliberately set himself to undermine it, that he had in particular urged on
his understrapper, Tickell, to get out a rival Homer.[3]
That Addison was not pleased to find himself so far
outstripped by someone sixteen years his junior, who
could no longer be flattered by kind encouragement,
nor be made the recipient of good advice, and that he
did not succeed in concealing his jealousy from the
sensitive Mr. Pope, seems highly probable. Whatever
the provocation, Pope set himself the task of making
ridiculous the gracious and gentle figure of a man all
but universally beloved. How should he do it? Had
he "called rogue and villain," however wittily, or even

fool, no one would have believed. Instead, with
diabolic cunning, he sought out the one spot of vul-
nerability in this so kindly nature, "bless'd with each
talent and each art to please." He found his "dram of
eale," "that little Speck, which all the rest will
spoil,"⁴ in a certain timidity and reserve and in a
rather complacent self-approbation:

> Should such a man, too fond to rule alone,
> Bear, like the Turk, no brother near the throne,
> View him with scornful, yet with jealous eyes,
> And hate for arts that caus'd himself to rise;
> Damn with faint praise, assent with civil leer,
> And without sneering, teach the rest to sneer;
> Willing to wound, and yet afraid to strike,
> Just hint a fault, and hesitate dislike;
>   . . .   .
> Like *Cato*, give his little Senate laws,
> And sit attentive to his own applause;
> While Wits and Templars ev'ry sentence raise,
> And wonder with a foolish face of praise—
> Who but must laugh, if such a man there be?
> Who would not weep, if ATTICUS were he?   (197-214)

Familiar as are the lines, they are of an art so perfect in every word and syllable that repeated quotation cannot stale them. With apparent candour,
Pope has granted all the virtues which made Addison
beloved; but he has so devised his portrait that all
these virtues shall take corruption from the stamp of
one defect. And Pope has not been unjust to Addison,
save in the very important articles of emphasis and
proportion. The one defect was really there; did not
the dying Addison, with a most unchristian self-
complacency, send for his stepson to see in what peace

a Christian can die? The defect once pointed out, one becomes aware of a timid complacency, and of an intellectual and moral priggishness, which mars, however slightly, the grace and charm of Addison's limpid prose. One wishes, but in vain, that Mr. Spectator should on some question or other speak out loud and bold. And so Pope's satirical portrait has over and above its other qualities become a real contribution to the literary appraisal of his one-time friend.

By a very different method, but with no less brilliant success, Pope solved the very delicate problem of holding up to ridicule the dull incompetence of no less a person than his sovereign lord, George II. When he chose to pillory Addison, he had to take into account prestige of character and personality; with George Augustus there was no prestige other than that which hedges in a king. But an English subject, least of all a barely tolerated "Papist," could not in so many words call fool and rogue, however wittily, to his king. Artistic restraint was powerfully reinforced by considerations of a more practical order. But loyal subjects have, time out of mind, addressed to their rulers flattery of the most exaggerated sort; all that was necessary was to direct the flattery towards aspects of George's character in which he was glaringly deficient, disguising the scandal in praise most obviously undeserved. Horace, in the First Epistle of the Second Book, had paid glowing, and in the main fully deserved, tribute to the great Augustus, as soldier, statesman, and patron of letters. George Augustus, stupid, indolent, totally lacking

in literary interests or tastes, was in character and
career as far removed as one could well imagine from
Cæsar Augustus. With devastating ingenuity, Pope
in his own *Epistle to Augustus* has paraphrased and
adapted Horace's glowing lines, and has readdressed
them to that monarch who is probably the least
edifying personage in all the annals of British royalty,
with only the most delicate insinuation that his
tongue is in his poetic cheek:

> Besides, a fate attends on all I write,
> That when I aim at praise, they say I bite.
> A vile Encomium doubly ridicules.　　　(408-10)

And Pope has heaped his double ridicule with complete immunity from any possibility of prosecution.
To accuse Pope of the crime of lese majesty, the
accuser must himself commit the same offence.

IV

Satire may ally itself to almost any literary form—
the drama as with Aristophanes and Molière and Mr.
Bernard Shaw; the novel as in Fielding's *Jonathan
Wild* or Samuel Butler's *Way of All Flesh*; the
ironical argument, or *reductio ad absurdum*, as in
Erasmus's *Praise of Folly* or Swift's *Argument against
Abolishing Christianity*. Three forms have proved
themselves particularly well adapted to serve as the
vehicle for satire: the fanciful tale, the mock-heroic
poem, and the epistle or imaginary dialogue in verse.

The fanciful tale traces back its pedigree to the
Veracious History of Lucian. With Lucian one sails
away to the Western Islands and thence to the Moon;

with Swift one visits Lilliput and Brobdingnag and the republic of horses; with Samuel Butler (second of the name) one crosses a high range of mountains and finds oneself in the moral topsy-turvydom of Erewhon. And everywhere one sees human beings, or some equivalent race, whose manners and customs, realistically described, are the satiric counterpart of our own.

The mock-heroic poem, exemplified in the delicate perfection of the *Rape of the Lock* and the splendid vigour of the *Dunciad*, has already been discussed in other chapters of this essay.

The traditional form of Roman satire is the epistle or imaginary dialogue in verse. It is when the laughter of rebuke so expresses itself that it most completely deserves the appellation of "a satire." Such a poem is in the critic's mind when he speaks of "formal satire." The primitive Latin *satura*, which was developed by Ennius and Lucilius and perfected by Horace and Juvenal, seems to have been in its origin rudely dramatic, a comic interlude without a plot, something analogous to the dialogue of question and answer carried on by the end-men of an old-fashioned minstrel show, with pointed hints at conspicuous personages of the community. This tradition of a dramatic origin was preserved by Horace in about half of his satires by the adoption of the form of the dialogue. Pope, who deliberately modeled his form on that of Horace, though he called his masterpiece in satire an *epistle* to Dr. Arbuthnot, actually made of it a dialogue between himself and his friend, in which,

however, Pope monopolizes all but a half dozen lines
of the conversation. The satire addressed to Mr.
Fortescue, and the two parts of *Seventeen Hundred
and Thirty Eight*, now known as the *Epilogue to the
Satires*, also take on the form of dialogue.

Even when dialogue proper is not used, it is as
though the poet were speaking to an imaginary com-
panion; and the style, both of Pope and Horace, is
always colloquial and familiar. Horace called his
satires *sermones*, discourses or conversations, and
pitched their tone accordingly. They never rise into
the higher regions of the grand manner. Neither in
substance nor in style is there any marked difference
between the collection of *sermones* and the equally
colloquial *epistolae*. Persius affected a studied harshness and obscurity of manner, a quality imitated with
no happy result by such early English practitioners
of formal satire as Bishop Hall and Dr. Donne.

Formal satire, so congenial to eighteenth-century
taste, is no longer in fashion; the satire which is being
written so lavishly by our own generation is more
often in prose than in verse—the cool prose of drama
and novel. Not a few modern readers, I imagine,
would think that the temper of satire is alien to that
of poetry. Satiric verse will conform but shabbily to
any definition of poetry laid down by critics of pro-
nouncedly romanticist leanings. It is, of course,
poetry of the judgment rather than of emotion, of
criticism rather than of creation. Its right to a place
on the slopes of Parnassus will stand or fall with that

of any poetry which is avowedly didactic. Yet one can hardly be satisfied with any attempted definition of poetry which should exclude the satiric verse of Horace and Boileau, of Dryden and Pope, of the Byron of *English Bards and Scotch Reviewers*. The realm of satire may be on the lower slopes of Parnassus; it may be a realm of silver rather than of gold; but its bards hold, none the less, in fealty to Apollo. If it does not demand creative imagination of the more exalted order, great satire does at least demand something of vision and an abundance of fertile wit and nimble fancy. It would be a barren sort of criticism which should spend much time debating the right of satire to assume poetic raiment; it is more profitable to ask what satire may gain from the use of verse. And the gain has been considerable. Verse-form gives it greater intensity, greater elevation, puts it farther from the mere calling of names, gives its blade a finer edge. Its need of terse, poignant expression was admirably served by the concise, highly disciplined, epigrammatic couplet of which Pope was so complete a master. In the closing paragraph of the *Dunciad*, and in the impassioned "triumph of vice" which concludes Dialogue I of the *Epilogue to the Satires*, Pope's satire has risen to a poetic level which is not far removed from the sublime:

> Lo! at the wheels of her Triumphal Car,
> Old England's Genius, rough with many a Scar,
> Dragg'd in the dust! his arms hang idly round,
> His Flag inverted trails along the ground!
> Our Youth, all liv'ry'd o'er with foreign Gold,
> Before her dance: behind her, crawl the Old!

See thronging Millions to the Pagod run,
And offer Country, Parent, Wife, or Son!
Hear the black Trumpet thro' the Land proclaim,
That NOT TO BE CORRUPTED IS THE SHAME.

V

When in the mid-summer of 1714, Queen Anne, after having entrusted the lord treasurer's staff to the whig Duke of Shrewsbury and so ensured the Hanoverian Succession, breathed her weary last, public confidence in the new dynasty immediately reflected itself in a considerable rise in the market value of the stocks. The stock-market boom of August, 1714, has all the significance of a symbol. Under the first two Georges and their whig ministers, particularly during the long ministry of Walpole, the industrial and mercantile development of England, begun at the Revolution, went forward with ever-accelerating momentum. The more stable values of landed property steadily receded in relative importance, as the speculative values of trade and stock-jobbing took first place in the national life. A great many people in England were getting rich very quickly indeed, to the accompaniment of those demoralizing influences which the process normally engenders. The famous South Sea Bubble which burst so disastrously in 1720 was but an exaggerated symptom of the national temper. Its bursting ushered in the more sound and sober, but equally sordid, régime of Robert Walpole. To Walpole's bitter critics—and among them were included most of the finer minds of his generation—it seemed that for him money was the only thing that mattered, that at his Midas-touch all that should have sustained the higher life of the nation was being transmuted into sordid gold.

To Pope and Swift and Arbuthnot and their like the passing of Queen Anne came as the death-knell of the England of their loyal love. The rest of their lives was to be spent in the opposition, and their chief weapon was the "sacred weapon, left for truth's defence," the barbed dart of satire.

As the twenty-odd years of Walpole's rule dragged on, Pope's attention was increasingly centered on England's besetting sin of avarice. In the days of Queen Anne he had made merry in the *Rape of the Lock* with the little follies and foibles of a highly sophisticated society in which he saw no evil more serious than triviality and misplaced emphasis. It is playful comedy, with only a modicum of kindly rebuke. In the *Dunciad* of 1728 and 1729, he is concerned with a more serious matter, the misdirection of human intelligence. One will hardly call the *Dunciad* gentle or kindly satire; but both in its more boisterous and its more subtle passages there is a certain measure of forbearance. Dulness, and pedantry, and misguided taste one can afford to combat with scorn rather than with the ardour of moral indignation. Avarice and corruption are a deadlier menace than pedantic dulness; and Pope's satire in the year 1738 has behind it the drive of a moral

earnestness which in 1728 showed itself only now and
then. And with the heightened earnestness goes a
heightened courage. The victims of the *Dunciad* were
for the most part denizens of Grub-street, persons of
no great social importance, who could strike back
with nothing more formidable than dull abuse; the
later satires attack the rich and powerful. In the
Epistle to Dr. Arbuthnot the kindly physician counsels
Pope:

> Good Friend, forbear! you deal in dang'rous things.
> I'd never name Queens, Ministers, or Kings;   (75-6)

but Pope does not forbear.

Avarice in its dual manifestation as niggardly par-
simony and vulgar prodigality, corruption in high
places, the wrong use of wealth and power, and contrasting praise of frugal temperance and old-fashioned
virtue are the theme of no less than nine of the satires
and epistles published between December, 1731, and
July, 1738. First of the series is the fourth *Moral
Essay*, which castigates the bad taste of the lavish
prodigality of "Timon's villa." A year later (January
15, 1733) Pope returns to the attack, and with greatly
heightened vigour, in the third *Moral Essay*, "Of the
Use of Riches." Here the question is not one of taste
but of the evils of misused wealth, as they affect the
character and the happiness of the individual, or
spread corruption through the corporate life of the
nation. There is the miserly "Cotta" whose graceless
heir scatters all in mad profusion, with the contrasting portrait of the "Man of Ross" who with a bare five

hundred pounds a year is the wise benefactor of a
whole countryside. There is "great Villiers," once
"lord of useless thousands," now ruined by the
prodigality of his vices, dying "in the worst inn's
worst room." There is finally Sir Balaam, stock-
jobber and director, progressively more corrupt and
unprincipled as his fortunes prosper, until at last, his
infamy exposed,

> The Devil and the King divide the prize,
> And sad Sir Balaam curses God and dies.   (401-2)

In November of the same year comes the "versification" of Dr. Donne's fourth satire, "The Impertinent," which exposes the general futility and corruption of the court. In the next July, the *Epistle to
Bethel* celebrates the temperate and frugal life[5]—

> What, and how great, the Virtue and the Art
> To live on little with a chearful heart.   (1-2)

In April, 1735 the "versification" of Dr. Donne's
second satire develops the theme—

> One, one man only breeds my just offence;
> Whom crimes gave wealth, and wealth gave Impudence.
>   (45-6)

During the years 1735-1737 other themes emerge in
the *Epistle to Dr. Arbuthnot*, which returns to the war
with the Dunces, and in the *Epistle to Augustus*. Then
in 1738 Pope returns to the subject of riches and
power. The "nil admirari" *Epistle to Murray* (published January 23) shows the futility of caring too
much for the things which wealth and influence can
give. The *Epistle to Bolingbroke* (March 7) once more

praises the life of wisdom and virtue as opposed to riches and worldly pomp:

> What right, what true, what fit, we justly call,
> Let this be all my care—for this is All.   (19-20)

In May and July appeared the two dialogues of *Seventeen Hundred and Thirty Eight*, now known as the *Epilogue to the Satires*, in which Pope's attack on corruption in high places glows with the ardour of a deep moral indignation, but none the less does not forget that satire must barb its darts with brilliant wit.

The seven years which begin with "Timon's villa" and end with the *Epilogue to the Satires* are, by virtue of Pope's great achievement, the golden age of formal satire in English. These satires and closely related epistles, varying in tone from light Horatian badinage to a zealous indignation which suggests the moral earnestness, though not the fierce intemperance, of Juvenal, written in a poetic style sometimes colloquial, sometimes eloquent, always vigorous yet urbane, are certainly unequalled by any other body of writings in their kind in the whole pageant of English literature. Pope's nearest rivals would be Dryden and Byron; but they are rivals *longo intervallo*. Nor would it be easy to find Pope's equal in satiric art in literatures other than English. Pope owes much to Horace, both in manner and in the substance of his avowed imitations; but the pupil has, I think, outrun his master. Pope's adaptation has made of the *Epistle to Augustus* something much more brilliant than Horace's original. And which of the satires or epistles of Horace can equal the artistic perfection of the *Epistle to Dr. Arbuthnot*, or the disciplined fervour of the *Epilogue to the Satires*? We cannot read them today with the zest which they had for those first readers who needed no footnotes to elucidate the personalities; but we of the twentieth century need no exegesis to make us understand the perverse corruptions of literary taste, or the sordid vulgarity and moral disintegration which may be the concomitants of material prosperity.

THE DUNCIAD OF 1743

THE many issues of the *Dunciad Variorum* during
the year 1729 were apparently sufficient to meet
the public demand for some time to come. It was not
printed again until 1735, when it was included in
"The Works of Mr. Alexander Pope. Volume II"
published in April of that year by Lawton Gilliver,[1]
and reprinted in 1736 and 1739. There were separate
issues in 1735 and 1741. In these various reprintings
there are minor revisions both in the poem and in the
accompanying annotations.

On March 20, 1742, was published by T. Cooper,
"at the *Globe* in Pater-noster Row," a handsomely
printed thin quarto of 48 pages entitled "The New
Dunciad: As it was Found In the Year 1741." Before
the end of the year it was reissued in five authorized,
and two probably pirated, London editions and in two
Dublin editions. Many readers must have been ready
to pay eighteen pence for a new *Dunciad*. There were
618 lines of text and a generous supply of "Remarks"
by Scriblerus at the foot of the page. An address "To
the Reader" gives this account of the new discovery:

> We apprehend it can be deemed no Injury to the
> Author of the *Three first Books* of the *Dunciad*, that
> we publish this *Fourth*. It was found merely by Ac-
> cident, in taking a Survey of the *Library* of a late

eminent Nobleman; but in so blotted a condition, and in so many detached pieces, as plainly shewed it to be not only *incorrect* but *unfinished*: That the Author of the three first Books had a design to extend and complete his Poem in this manner, appears from the Dissertation prefixt to it, where it is said, that *the Design is more extensive, and that we may expect other Episodes to complete it*: And from the Declaration in the Argument to the third Book,[2] that *the Accomplishment of the Prophecies therein, would be the Theme hereafter of a Greater Dunciad*. But whether or no he be the Author of this, we declare ourselves ignorant.

This newly discovered "Book the Fourth" gives us, then, the "accomplishment of the prophecy" at the end of Book III that universal darkness shall blot out all enlightenment. As the "Argument" of the new fourth book puts it, the poet "shews the Goddess coming in her Majesty to destroy *Order* and *Science*, and to substitute the *Kingdom of the Dull* upon earth."

It is only by the slender thread of a prophecy fulfilled that Book IV is organically joined to what precedes. The action of the mock epic had been in the previous books somewhat desultory; in the fourth book there is, properly speaking, no action at all. But if in this respect inferior, the fourth book shows no falling off in the vigour of its satirical poetry. Madness, dulness, and a perverted taste now reign supreme. The nine Muses have been displaced by the "Harlot form" of Italian opera. All the tribes of the Dull "cohere around" about the Goddess—

Not closer, orb in orb, conglob'd are seen
The buzzing Bees about their dusky Queen.

(IV, 79-80)

The fourth book deals more with the several categories of dulness, and much less than do its predecessors with individual exemplifying Dunces. The chief
emphasis of the satire is directed at the system of
education in school and college which, itself a
triumph of dulness, may be trusted to perpetuate this
triumph to all the generations still unborn. The
Genius of the Schools proudly proclaims to the Goddess and to her assembled host of Dunces his whole
theory of education:

Since Man from beast by Words is known,
Words are Man's province, Words we teach alone.
. . .   .
We ply the Memory, we load the brain,
Bind rebel Wit, and double chain on chain;
Confine the thought, to exercise the breath;
And keep them in the pale of Words till death.
Whate'er the talents, or howe'er design'd,
We hang one jingling padlock on the mind.

(IV, 149-62)

And the professors of this educational program form
before our eyes into an academic procession:

Prompt at the call, around the Goddess roll
Broad hats, and hoods, and caps, a sable shoal:
Thick and more thick the black blockade extends,
A hundred head of Aristotle's friends.   (IV, 189-92)

The "sable shoal" of the academic procession is rudely
pushed aside by the "gay embroider'd race" of the
parade of returning alumni, the young gentlemen

who, having been nurtured on Words, have completed
their education by a grand tour of Europe:

> Thro' School and College, thy kind cloud o'ercast,
> Safe and unseen the young Æneas past.
> Thence bursting glorious, all at once let down,
> Stunn'd with his giddy Larum half the town;
> Intrepid then, o'er seas and lands he flew,
> Europe he saw, and Europe saw him too.
>
> . . .   .
>
> Saw ev'ry Court, heard ev'ry King declare
> His royal Sense of Op'ras or the Fair;
> The Stews and Palace equally explor'd,
> Intrigu'd with glory, and with spirit whor'd;
> Try'd all *hors-d'œuvres*, all *liqueurs* defin'd,
> Judicious drank, and greatly-daring din'd.
>
> (IV, 289-92, 313-18)

If any more serious interests have been awakened,
they are the shallow interests of the antiquary, the
virtuoso, and the "minute philosopher," who never
"proceed beyond *Trifles*, to any useful or extensive
views of Nature, or of the Author of Nature."[3]

When Pope was telling Spence (p. 315) of the ambitious plan of a great "ethic work" of which the
Essay on Man was to have been the first book, he
explained that the second book "would have been on
Knowledge and its limits:—here would have come in
an Essay on Education; part of which I have inserted
in the Dunciad." It is the most brilliant and memorable part of the fourth book, and shows Pope's satiric
art at its most vigorous pitch.

It was in the year 1743 that the *Dunciad* took on its
final form. On October 29 of that year was published

by M. Cooper, "at the Globe in Pater-noster-row," a substantial quarto of 258 pages, priced at 7s. 6d., with the title: "The Dunciad in Four Books. Printed according to the complete Copy found in the Year 1742." The three books of the earlier *Dunciad* are now supplemented by the fourth book which had been published in the preceding year, and to the end of it has been transferred, with a few revisions, the splendid passage which had originally concluded Book III.[4] The most important innovation, however, is that the poem is now provided with a new hero. In the seventeen years that had elapsed since the publication of *Shakespeare Restored*, Theobald and his offensive book had faded into the background of Pope's consciousness, and for his readers (whom Pope never forgot) he had become an old story. So Theobald was dethroned from his bad eminence as anointed King of Dulness, and Colley Cibber, who in 1729 had been only a minor figure among the Dunces, was crowned in his stead.

Colley Cibber (1671-1757), now an elderly gentleman of seventy-two, had been since the last decade of the seventeenth century a conspicuous figure in the theatrical world of London as patentee of the Theatre-Royal in Drury Lane, comic dramatist,[5] and actor in eccentric parts. Always a staunch Whig, he was appointed in 1730 Poet Laureate in succession to Laurence Eusden (Pope's "parson much bemused in beer"). The appointment was one of the least appropriate ever made to that office; for, whatever were Cibber's qualities as actor and dramatist, he was by

no stretch of the word to be accounted a poet. To
Pope such an appointment might well have seemed
the immediate fulfilment of the prophecy that Dulness was now to reign supreme. And Cibber was also
for Pope a striking embodiment of the low estate of
contemporary drama.

In 1740 Cibber delivered himself bound into the
hands of all his detractors by publishing in a very
handsome large quarto volume, with his engraved
portrait as frontispiece, an autobiography entitled
"An Apology for the Life of Mr. Colley Cibber,
Comedian, and Late Patentee of the Theatre-Royal.
With an Historical View of the Stage during his Own
Time. Written by Himself." The very title of the book
was an invitation to ridicule,[6] as, indeed, was the unfortunate collocation of syllables which made up its
author's name. Cibber's book is actually a very entertaining book, written in racy though often "incorrect"
English,[7] and invaluable for the light which it throws
on the history of the London stage. It is lively (Pope
would have said "pert"), very vain and very impudent; but the impudence is so good-natured, and
the vanity so naïvely frank, that the modern reader
is diverted rather than annoyed.

In Chapter II of his *Apology* (p. 22) Cibber has
this to say of Pope, who had since 1728 been making
free with his name:

> When I therefore find my Name at length, in the
> Satyrical Works of our most celebrated living Author,
> I never look upon those Lines as Malice meant to me,
> (for he knows I never provok'd it) but Profit to him-
> self: One of his Points must be, to have many Readers:

He considers that my Face and Name are more known than those of many thousands of more consequence in the Kingdom: That therefore, right or wrong, a Lick at the Laureat will always be a sure Bait, *ad captandum vulgus*, to catch him little Readers: And that to gratify the Unlearned, by now and then interspersing those merry Sacrifices of an old Acquaintance to their Taste, is a piece of quite right Poetical Craft.

This good-natured protest of Cibber did not deter Pope from taking a fresh fling at him in the "New Dunciad" of 1742 in the line—

Soft on her Lap her Laureat son reclines,

to which Scriblerus provides a long footnote in which is quoted part of the passage printed above from the *Apology*.

The "New Dunciad" had been published on March 20. A few months later appeared a shilling pamphlet, dated "July the 7th 1742," with this title: "A Letter from Mr. Cibber, to Mr. Pope, Inquiring into the Motives that might induce him in his Satyrical Works, to be so frequently fond of Mr. Cibber's Name." Cibber had, he says, in the *Apology* "offer'd him a friendly release of all Damages" (p. 7), but Pope has refused the proffered olive branch; in "your last new *Dunciad* . . . you still seem to enjoy your so often repeated Glory of being bright upon my Dulness." (p. 6.) Cibber maintains throughout the letter a certain light-hearted gaiety of manner; but he says things that Pope could not have enjoyed reading, the most objectionable being an anecdote, dug up from many years ago, which exhibits young Mr. Pope in an amorous adventure that is both disreputable and humiliating.

When Pope in the "New Dunciad" placed the Laureate in the very lap of the Goddess Dulness, it is not unlikely that he was already meditating the deposition of King Theobald and the elevation of Cibber. If so, the Laureate had now given him provocation sufficient to justify the attack. One is tempted to think that Pope may have deliberately provoked the provocation. For if the poem was to be revamped, where could one have found a better hero than the Poet Laureate. As the anonymous author of a pamphlet called *A Blast upon Bays*[8] says to him:

> You are a Dunce of such Importance, as to wear the only Laurel of the Kingdom interwoven with your Poppies. To be the titular Monarch of Wit, and receive a Salary in that Capacity; must it not make Folly the more egregious, where it was before remarkable. (p. 6)

And so Dunce the second reigned in place of Dunce the first. In the "Advertisement to the Reader," signed "W. W." prefixed to "The Dunciad in Four Books," Dr. Warburton gives this account of the matter:[9]

> I had lately the pleasure to pass some months with the Author in the Country. . . . It happen'd, that just at that juncture was published a ridiculous book against him, full of Personal Reflections which furnished him with a lucky opportunity of improving *This Poem*, by giving it the only thing it wanted, a *more considerable Hero*. He was always sensible of its defect in that particular, and owned he had let it pass

with the Hero it had, purely for want of a better; not entertaining the least expectation that such an one was reserved for this Post, as has since obtained the *Laurel*: But since that had happened, he could no longer deny this justice either to *him* or the *Dunciad*.

In the *Dunciad* of 1729 it was chiefly in the first book that King Theobald had occupied the centre of attention. The substitution for him of King Colley involved, therefore, a considerable revision of Book I. In Books II and III, on the other hand, hardly any alterations were necessary; such occasional revisions as there are make no essential change in the substance of the poem, and a great many lines show no alteration whatever. In Book I the revision is not carried through with complete consistency. Many fine lines, too brilliant to be sacrificed in a revision, which had been highly appropriate when applied to Theobald, are retained though much of their point has been lost.

Cibber himself promptly pointed out these inconsistencies. In January, 1743, he published "Another Occasional Letter From Mr. Cibber To Mr. Pope"— this time a thoroughly angry letter, with all pretense of good-natured toleration thrown to the winds—in the course of which he says:

> The bare Change of one Name for another is his whole Expence of Thought about it! The Materials, and Furniture of the Character, even to the same Books, in his Study (which he knew would never be look'd into) stand just in their old Places! the Clouds, the Mists, the Fogs, and same Vapours of Dullness (let them never so much obscure the Likeness) will serve for any Mortal he has a mind to wrap in them!

> therefore stand clear, good People! for when *Pope* is
> in a blind Passion, no Body knows who may feel the
> Effect on't! (p. 29)

And in the same "Letter," Cibber asks what may
have been Pope's motive in revamping his poem. Was
it resentment at Cibber's earlier "Letter" of more
than a year ago?

> I doubt I have so offended the Gravity, and Great-
> ness of your Soul, that to secure your more ample
> Revenge, you have prudently taken the full term of
> thirteen months Consideration, before you would
> pour it, upon me! But at last, it seems, we have it, and
> now Souse! out comes your old *Dunciad*, in a new
> Dress, like fresh Gold, upon stale Ginger-bread, sold
> out, in Penny-worth's of shining King *Colley*, crown'd
> the Hero of Immortal Stupidity. (p. 8)

Or is there another reason, one dictated not by
Pope's emotions but by the prudent calculation of an
author always mindful of his audience and of his own
pecuniary profit?

> Come! shall I give you a merrier Excuse, tho' per-
> haps your Gravity won't so well like it? To say, then,
> that you did it, with an eye to your getting off another
> Edition of your Book. . . . (p. 14)

I think that in suggesting this "excuse," Mr. Colley
Cibber came very near the truth. There had been, it
seems, a brisk demand for the "New Dunciad" of
1742. Had Pope merely added this fourth book to the
other three, such a "Dunciad in Four Books" would
have been only a reissue of old matter. Is it, perhaps,
significant that in 1743 fourteen years had elapsed
since the *Dunciad* of 1729, and that the copyright on

it had consequently expired? Here was a chance to produce, with comparatively little effort, a new book which could be sold for seven shillings, sixpence.

However profitable the procedure may have been to Pope's pocketbook, I think there can be no question that, artistically, Pope's judgment was at fault in thus remaking his book. The fourth book contains, to be sure, some of his most vigorous and effective satire; but it is only very loosely joined to the preceding books, and action there is none at all. The added book is merely a brilliant supplement; and, extending as it does to 656 lines, it is out of proportion with those which go before. In 1729 the poem was but a little over a thousand lines in length. In 1743 there are more than 1,750 lines, and that is, I think, too long for a poem of this character. Many a modern reader has doubtless been deterred from undertaking the reading of it by its imposing bulk of poetry and satirical commentary. It is a pity that Pope could not have been content to let his poem stand as it appeared in 1729, and to have made not a "Book the Fourth," but an independent poem out of the "New Dunciad, as it was Found In the Year 1741."

The *Dunciad* of 1743 was to be the final accomplishment of Pope's Muse. Such failing energy as he could command in the seven months of life that were left for him was spent in revising poetry already written. He died on May 30, 1744, having duly received the last sacraments from a priest of the Roman Catholic

Church. Spence records that "his departure was so easy, that it was imperceptible even to the standers by." He was cured at last of that "long disease, his life"; but English literature had lost one of its major poets. Between the death of Dryden in 1700 and the emergence of Wordsworth and Coleridge in 1798, he is the only English poet for whom we can confidently predict a continuing memory of poetic fame.

BIBLIOGRAPHICAL NOTE

THE established edition of Pope's *Works* is still that of Elwin and Courthope in ten volumes, London, 1871-1889, which, however, does not include the translations of Homer. In spite of serious inadequacies of method and of a bias curiously hostile to Pope both as man and as poet, it contains much material indispensable to a serious student. The best complete edition of Pope's poetry within small compass is that in the Cambridge Poets series, edited by H. W. Boynton, Houghton Mifflin Company, Boston and New York, 1903, which includes the whole of the *Iliad* and those books of the *Odyssey* for which Pope was primarily responsible. An excellent volume of selections, provided with thoroughly sound introductions, is edited by George Sherburn for Thomas Nelson and Sons, New York, 1929. A new edition of Pope's works in several volumes is announced for publication by Basil Blackwell, at Oxford, of which one volume, containing the earlier prose works edited by Norman Ault (1936), has appeared.

The Early Career of Alexander Pope by George Sherburn, Oxford, 1934, is an admirable study, sympathetic yet judicial, and based on a wealth of new materials, of Pope's life until the year 1726. It is greatly to be hoped that Professor Sherburn will deal in similar fashion with the later career of Pope. The Life by Sir Leslie Stephen, English Men of Letters series, London, 1880, is written from the standpoint of marked hostility to Pope; much more friendly is the Life by W. J. Courthope in Volume V of the Elwin-Courthope edition. *Mr. Pope* by "George Paston" (Miss E. M. Symonds), 2 vols., London, 1909, is marred by serious inaccuracies. Miss Edith Sitwell's *Alexander Pope*, London, 1930, is very readable, but not always trustworthy. Miss Sitwell's laudation of Pope's character is in pleasant contrast with Sir Leslie Stephen's equally uncritical condemnation.

Of first-rate importance and quite indispensable to serious students is Professor R. H. Griffith's *Alexander Pope, a Bibliography*, 2 vols., Austin, Texas, 1922 and 1927, which lists and analyzes in full detail all publications of Pope's writings through and including the year 1751. A third volume is promised which will deal with contemporary writings about Pope. Other books of importance are *Alexander Pope as Critic and Humanist* by Austin Warren, Princeton, 1929, and *L'Influence française dans l'œuvre de Pope* by E. Audra, Paris, 1931. Geoffrey Tillotson's *On the Poetry of Pope*, Oxford, 1938, is a penetrating study of Pope's technical mastery in language and verse.

Quotations from the poems of Pope are in every case from early editions, the typographical peculiarities of which have been scrupulously preserved. Poems which were included in the collected edition of 1717 are quoted from the folio of that year. Quotations from the *Iliad* are from the subscribers' edition in quarto of 1715-1720. The *Dunciad* of 1729 is quoted from the quarto of that year; the fourth book of the *Dunciad* is quoted from the quarto of 1743. Other quotations from Pope's poetry are from Warburton's edition of 1751. Pope's correspondence is quoted from the text of the Elwin-Courthope edition. Joseph Spence's *Anecdotes, Observations, and Characters of Books and Men*, which contains records of Pope's conversation, is quoted from Singer's text, London, 1820.

NOTES

NOTES TO CHAPTER I

[1] This quotation and those which precede it are from the early paragraphs (pp. ii-v) of Pope's Preface to his edition of Shakespeare (1725). For a detailed discussion of Pope's edition of Shakespeare and of the critical judgments contained in it, see Austin Warren, *Alexander Pope as Critic and Humanist*, Princeton, 1929, Chapter IV.

[2] Spence, p. 332, and Warburton's note to Pope's first letter to Wycherley, Elwin-Courthope, VI, 15.

[3] Quoted by C. F. E. Spurgeon, *Five Hundred Years of Chaucer Criticism and Allusion*, I, 289.

[4] R. D. Havens, *The Influence of Milton on English Poetry*, Cambridge [Mass.], 1922, pp. 113-18, 573-83.

[5] The Huntington Library owns a thin quarto volume entitled: "*The Art of Poetry*, written in French by The Sieur de Boileau, made English by Sir William Solmes. London, Printed for R. Bentley, and S. Magnes, in Russel-street in Covent Garden, 1683." On the fly-leaf is written in a very neat round hand: "Alexander Pope" followed by "Pretm 8d." Pope may well have made this eight-penny purchase during the early years at Binfield. In the lower margins of Cantos I and IV Pope has in a very neat printing hand analyzed Boileau's matter. In Canto I the annotations, which extend from page 1 to page 11, read: "Precept I. Not to write without a Genius. Precept II. To know your Talent. III. Sence the Rule of all Writing, Reason the Guide. IV. Against Impertinent Descriptions. V. Variety of Style. VI. Against Meanness of Style. VII. Correct Versification. VIII. Agst Obscurity. IX. Purity of Language. X. Not to write fast. XI. Disposition and Design. XII. Submission to able Judges." In the lower margins of pages 54-61 one reads: "Canto IV. This canto contains Advice to Poets, in regard to their Conduct. I. That there is no Medium in Poetry. II. How far to submit to Correction of Criticks. [III is left out.] IV. The Morals a Poet ought to have. V. Agst the mercenary Temper of some Authors."

[6] For a very thorough discussion of the fundamental principles which were involved in the controversy, see R. F. Jones, *Ancients and Moderns* (Washington University Studies), St. Louis, 1936.

[7] La Motte, *Discours sur Homère* (1714): Des Dieux, Des Héros.

[8] The date of Walsh's death, according to modern reckoning, is March 18, 1708; but if the new year is begun with Ladyday (March 25), his death falls at the very end of 1707. There is, thus, no inconsistency in Pope's statement to Spence.

[9] Ed. 1711, p. 3. Dennis proceeds to quote, by way of proving that Pope is "a slave to Authority and Opinion," the lines of the *Essay* which begin "Still

Green with Bays each ancient Altar stands" (181-200). Again on p. 29 Dennis repeats the attack:

> This little Author may extol the Ancients as much and as long as he pleases, but he has reason to thank the good Gods that he was born a Modern. For had he been born of *Græcian* Parents, and his Father by consequence had by Law the absolute Disposal of him, his Life had been no longer than that of one of his poems,—the Life of half a day.

Is Dennis here more concerned to attack Pope's critical position or to be brutally witty at the expense of his poor shrunken crippled body?

[10] The word "fancy" occurs only once in the *Essay* (line 667); "imagination" also appears but once (line 58).

[11] Pope uses the word "imagination" as a synonym for "invention" in the paragraphs of the Preface in which he discusses Homer's images and his expression. The word "wit" is not used in the Preface.

NOTES TO CHAPTER II

[1] Perhaps one should add *The Dying Christian to his Soul* and "Happy the man."

[2] Elwin-Courthope, IX, 14.

[3] See Austin Warren, *Alexander Pope as Critic and Humanist*, Princeton, 1929, pp. 263-4, 270.

[4] Brit. Mus. Egerton 1950. Professor Edward Snyder has reprinted the text in *Journal of English and Germanic Philology*, XVIII, 583 (1919).

[5] One might add *Two Chorus's to the Tragedy of Brutus* first published in the collected *Works* of 1717.

[6] The letter and the date have only the authority of the 1735 edition of Pope's letters. It is substantially the same as Pope's letter to Cromwell of Dec. 5, 1710, for which the original has survived. See Elwin-Courthope, VI, 56-9, 111-14.

[7] The following statistical table may serve to indicate the range of this variation. The percentages given must be considered approximations, since it is not likely that any two readers will precisely agree on the proper metrical interpretation of every individual line. For purposes of comparison I have added figures for passages from Waller, Denham, and Dryden, who were Pope's acknowledged masters in his metrical apprenticeship.

	Normal	Light	Heavy
Autumn (complete)	63%	20%	17%
Rape of the Lock (III, 1-100)	57%	34%	9%
Iliad (VI, 580-679)	54%	34%	12%
Eloisa (207-306)	36%	31%	33%
Moral Essay IV (99-168)	34%	42%	24%
Arbuthnot (1-100)	23%	52%	25%

Dunciad (IV, 1-100)	46%	28%	26%
Waller, To the King on his Navy (complete)	65%	32%	3%
Denham, *Cooper's Hill* (1-100)	60%	32%	8%
Dryden, *Hind and Panther* (I, 63-137)	62%*	28%	10%
Dryden, *Absalom and Achitophel* (I, 501-600)	40%	45%	15%

*This percentage includes three Alexandrines of completely normal type.

The varying ratio of these percentages suggests something of the varying modulations which Pope educed from his single pattern—the mellifluous sweetness of the *Pastorals* with its high percentage of normally stressed lines; the rapid flow of the *Iliad* with its preponderance of normal and light lines; the emotional elevation of *Eloisa* with its high proportion of heavy lines; the easy colloquial vigour of Pope's satiric verse, where the light line is the dominant type, as it is also in Dryden's satire. If one compares the percentages for Pope with those for his predecessors, the most striking divergence is his much greater use of the weighted line. I suspect that this element of Pope's metric may be due to the influence of Milton, in whose pentameter lines the heaping up of heavy syllables is a very characteristic trait.

[8] Dr. Johnson is our authority for this statement. *Lives of the English Poets*, ed. G. B. Hill, III, 250.

NOTES TO CHAPTER III

[1] Elwin-Courthope, IX, 545. I have taken the text, however, from Sherburn, p. 51, who has corrected the text from the original manuscript.

[2] The last page of the volume bears the page-number 751, but pp. 633-720 are non-existent, and there are other discrepancies in the pagination, all of which, curiously enough, concern Pope's contributions to the volume.

[3] The Fifth Part had been published in 1704. The "most eminent hands" were not very eminent. Wycherley was not exaggerating when he wrote to Pope on May 26, 1709: "The salt of your wit has been enough to give a relish to the whole inspid hotch-potch it is mingled with." The Miscellany contained, however, on pp. 237-48 Swift's *Baucis and Philemon*, but without the author's name.

[4] *Guardian*, No. 22, April 6, 1713. Quoted from the collected edition of 1714.

[5] Ed. 1717, p. 5 (Elwin-Courthope, I, 258).

[6] Creech's translation, pp. 51-2.

[7] *Ibid.*, pp. 38-9.

[8] *Works*, 1743, Vol. I, Part I, pp. 27-8.

[9] *Essay on the Writings and Genius of Pope* (1756), I, 2.

[10] I quote from the edition of 1751. Essentially the same note is found in the 1743 edition; but the latter part of the note is less clearly phrased. Both editions give the date 1710.

NOTES TO CHAPTER IV

1 In the collected edition of 1741 and in Warburton's edition of 1751 it is transferred to the volume of "Translations and Imitations."

2 The note is not in the edition of 1717 or in subsequent collected editions, including Warburton's. It is given in Elwin-Courthope, I, 205.

3 In *Poems on Several Occasions* (1717) there is on pages 107-8 a set of verses headed "To Belinda on the Rape of the Lock," which "salve the lady's honour, without affixing her name." Mr. Ault suggests, in the introduction to his facsimile reprint of this miscellany (1935), that these verses are the rejected preface.

4 Notes to *Epistle to Dr. Arbuthnot* in Warburton's ed. of 1751, IV, 26.

5 The *Lutrin* in four cantos was translated into English in 1682 by an unidentified "N.O." It is a rough and very free translation. Each canto has a prefixed "Argument" in Hudibrastic verse. The translation is in five-stress couplets, but with very frequent use of double rhymes, often of a grotesque character, which gives it a Hudibrastic flavour. The diction is highly colloquial.

6 For a valuable discussion of the mock-heroic, see R. P. Bond, *English Burlesque Poetry*, 1700-1750, Cambridge, Mass., 1932.

7 (Discourse II.) I quote from the translation of 1714, p. 21.

8 In the *Count of Gabalis* one reads: "These pretended Fairies were nothing but *Sylphids* and *Nymphs*." (Transl. 1714, p. 86.) There is nothing in the book to justify Pope's statement that the sylphs were "once inclos'd in Woman's beauteous mold"; nor that the sylphs, like Milton's fallen angels, can "assume what sexes and what shapes they please." Each of the four orders of Rosicrucian spirits includes male and female beings.

9 Thirty additional lines (V, 7-36) were added in 1717.

10 These two French artists were among the most distinguished illustrators of the day. In February, 1714 they were associated in producing a series of engraved plates illustrative of the battles of Marlborough and Prince Eugene. See *D.N.B. s. vv.*

11 Elwin-Courthope, IX, 359, 360, 361.

12 "Verses" was changed to "Elegy" in the edition of 1736.

13 Vol. I, pp. 75-6.

14 The whole matter was settled once for all by C. W. Dilke in the *Athenaeum* for July 15, 1854. Dilke's paper is reprinted in *Papers of a Critic*, I, 117-40.

15 *Writings and Genius of Pope* (1756), I, 253.

16 Elwin-Courthope, IX, 264. The letter is undated. It would seem to belong in 1716, perhaps in Holy Week.

17 That it was so regarded by contemporaries is shown by the fact that when in October, 1719, Lintot issued a "Second Edition" of *Eloisa to Abelard*, he accompanied it with the *Verses to an Unfortunate Lady*; "Florelio, a Pastoral on the death of the Marquis of Blandford" by Mr. Fenton; "Upon the Death of her Husband," by Mrs. Elizabeth Singer; and Allan Ramsay's

"Richy and Sandy, a Pastoral on the Death of Mr. Joseph Addison." The volume is dated 1720. It is a "second edition" because the poem had previously been printed in the *Works* of 1717.

[18] Petrarch owned a manuscript of the Latin *Letters*, now in the Bibliothèque Nationale, which contains marginal annotations in his own hand; and Villon includes "la très sage Héloys" in his *Ballade des Dames du temps jadis*. The letters were not printed until 1616. See C. Charrier, *Héloise dans l'histoire et dans la légende*, Paris, 1933, pp. 388-94, 403-6.

[19] The literary history of the French translation that goes under the name of Bussy-Rabutin is a complicated one. See C. Charrier, *op. cit.*, pp. 406-38, 605-13 and E. Audra, *L'Influence française dans l'œuvre de Pope*. Paris, 1931, pp. 403-26.

[20] I am not inclined to take seriously Savage's statement to Johnson that Pope's "first inclination to attempt a composition of that tender kind arose . . . from his perusal of Prior's *Nut-brown Maid*." See *Lives of the English Poets*, ed. G. B. Hill, III, 105.

[21] It is quite possible that the *Letters* are a work of fiction without foundation in actual fact.

[22] The Brit. Mus. Catalogue lists subsequent editions in 1686, 1693, and 1701.

[23] It is No. 28 in the Grolier Club catalogue of engraved portraits: *An Exhibition of the First Editions of the Works of Alexander Pope*. [New York], 1911.

NOTES TO CHAPTER V

[1] The pages of the Huntington Library copy measure 17½ x 11 inches. The title page in black and red reads: "Homer His Iliads Translated, Adorn'd with Sculpture, and Illustrated with Annotations, by John Ogilby. London, Printed by Thomas Roycroft, and are to be had at the Author's House in Kings-head Court within Shoe-Lane, MDCLX." There are 40 (unnumbered) pages of introductory matter and 518 pages of text and marginal annotations. Ogilby's *Odyssey* was published in 1665.

[2] Elwin-Courthope, VI, 3-4. The letter rests only on the authority of Pope's 1735 edition of his correspondence.

[3] Nichols, *Literary Anecdotes*, I, 76.

[4] Elwin-Courthope, V, 149.

[5] Nichols, *Literary Anecdotes*, VIII, 300. Compare Spence, p. 295.

[6] Pope's enemies were not slow to fling these handsome profits in his face. Early in 1715 was published a six-penny pamphlet entitled "Homerides: or, a Letter to Mr. Pope, Occasion'd by his intended Translation of Homer. By Sir Iliad Doggrel," which contains this sentence (p. 6): "There are indeed two Things to be considered in every Heroick Poem; first, how to *write* the Poem, secondly, how to make it *sell*." There are other jibes about Pope's "subscription money." For further attacks of this sort see Sherburn, *Early Career of Alexander Pope*, pp. 133-9.

⁷ Pope's debt to Broome and Parnell is duly acknowledged at the end of Volume VI. Both declined his offer of pecuniary reward.

⁸ I quote the lines (47-8) from the manuscript version as printed in G. C. Faber's edition of *The Poetical Works of John Gay*, pp. 667-70, where it bears the title "Alexander Pope his safe return from Troy."

⁹ Quoted by J. E. Spingarn in the Introduction to *Critical Essays of the Seventeenth Century*, I, lv. This section of Mr. Spingarn's Introduction gives an excellent résumé of "The Theory of Translation."

¹⁰ There are 15,694 lines in the Greek *Iliad* and 18,956 in Pope's translation. The percentage of increment varies a good deal from book to book, a variation from 11% in Book XIX, and 12% in Book XVII to 29% in Book XXII and 28% in Books I and VI. It may be remarked that the average number of syllables to a line in the Greek is about fifteen as compared with the all-but-uniform ten of the English.

¹¹ *Faery Queene*, I, xi, x.

¹² *Writings and Genius of Pope*, II (1782), 476.

¹³ *ibid.*, 296. If Warton's information is correct, the episode must have happened before Bishop Atterbury's arrest for treason in 1722. For a somewhat different version of the story dating from 1735, see Sherburn, *Early Career of Pope*, p. 265. Spondanus is Jean de Sponde, who in 1583 published an edition of Homer with a Latin translation and commentary.

¹⁴ Sir John Hawkins (*Works of Samuel Johnson* (1787), XI, 126, n.) is authority for this phrasing of Bentley's comment. It may be noted that Hawkins's version of the anecdote makes Bentley one of the subscribers to Pope's "Homer." His name, however, does not appear in the printed list of subscribers for the *Iliad* or for the *Odyssey*.

¹⁵ On June 8, 1715, just two days after the publication of the first volume of Pope's *Iliad*, was published by Lintot's rival, Jacob Tonson "at Shakespear's-Head over-against Catherine-street in the Strand" a rival translation of "The First Book of Homer's Iliad," by Thomas Tickell, a protegé of Addison. Mr. Tickell was a competent classical scholar and a respectable minor poet. His translation keeps closer to the original than does Pope's, and is less dressed up with "Ovidian graces"; but it is utterly unreadable. There is neither music nor fire in its couplets. Its only use is to send the reader back to Pope with heightened admiration for what Pope has done. For a detailed account of the matter, see Sherburn, *Early Career of Pope*, pp. 127-45. Professor Sherburn has shown good reason to believe that Tickell's publication immediately after that of Pope was deliberately devised to take the edge off of Pope's achievement, and that Addison was to some extent involved in the affair.

¹⁶ In the Preface to the *Iliad* (Fol. E 4, recto) Pope suggests that "perhaps the mixture of some *Græcisms* and old words after the manner of *Milton*, if done without too much Affectation, might not have an ill Effect in a Version of this particular Work." But of specifically Miltonic diction he has made only sparing use.

NOTES TO CHAPTER VI

[1] See R. H. Griffith, *Alexander Pope, a Bibliography*, Vol. I, Part I, pp. 165, 168 and the interesting article by S. R. Sutherland, *"The Dunciad* of 1729," *Modern Language Review*, XXXI, 347-53 (1936), which discusses the legal complications as to the copyright.

[2] Pope's name had appeared on a pirated Dublin print of the 1728 edition; but the work was not formally avowed until the *Dunciad* was included in the 1735 edition of Pope's collected *Works*.

[3] First Satire of the Second Book of Horace, line 116 (published in 1733).

[4] The inclusion of the *Bathos* in this volume would seem to have been an afterthought, not decided on until the rest of the volume was in type. On May 27 of the previous year, Pope and Swift, who was Pope's guest at Twickenham, had jointly signed their names to the Preface of "Miscellanies in Prose and Verse." They had come to the opinion "that the best Method we could take for justifying ourselves, would be to publish whatever loose Papers in Prose and Verse, we have formerly written." There were to be two, and perhaps three, volumes made up "of several small Treatises in Prose." The verses were to be "transferred into a Volume apart." Two volumes of prose were published in June, 1727. The promised volume of verse, "Miscellanies. The Last Volume. London: Printed for B. Motte, at the Middle Temple Gate Fleet-Street. 1727," did not appear until March 8, 1728. The *Bathos* is the first piece in this volume. It ends on p. 93, after which is a half-title, "Miscellanies in Verse," followed by Swift's *Cadenus and Vanessa* with fresh pagination (1-64). The pagination begins once more anew with *Baucis and Philemon* and continues thence unbroken to the end of the volume.

When, in 1732, the final volume of this series, confusingly entitled "Miscellanies. The Third Volume," appeared, it contained 276 pages of prose, followed, with new pagination, by 100 pages of verse. In the "Bookseller's Advertisement" we read: "The *Verses* are paged separately, that they may be added to that Volume which wholly consists of Verse, and the Treatise of the *Bathos* placed in their stead in This."

[5] Blackmore died October 9, 1729. The quotation is from Chapter VI.

[6] He has given a list of them on pages 91-3 of the "Dunciad Variorum."

[7] See Griffith, *Bibliography*, Vol. I, Part I, p. 152. A type facsimile of the octavo was published in 1928 by the Clarendon Press, Oxford.

[8] Elwin-Courthope, IV, 28. Another adjective frequently applied by Pope to the Duncas is *pert*, which is used to mean "self-confident"; "forward to express opinions, though not qualified to form them"; "impudent." Swift writes in the *Journal to Stella* on July 15, 1711: "We had a sad pert dull parson at Kensington to-day."

[9] *Epistle to Dr. Arbuthnot*, line 15.

[10] Notes to II, 266, 270.

[11] Spence, *Anecdotes*, p. 10. The fragmentary *Memoirs of Martinus Scriblerus*, in which Pope and Arbuthnot, and perhaps others, had a hand, was first printed in the octavo edition of Pope's *Works* published in 1742. It is a

satire primarily on the "projects" of natural philosophers, similar in tone to the third voyage of *Gulliver*. Chapter IX, however, deals with textual criticism.

[12] David Mallet has this to say of Bentley in his poem, "Of Verbal Criticism: An Epistle to Mr. Pope. Occasioned by Theobald's Shakespear, and Bentley's Milton . . . 1733":

> While *Bentley*, long to wrangling schools confin'd,
> And but by books acquainted with mankind,
> Dares, in the fulness of the Pedant's pride,
> Rhime tho' no genius, tho' no judge decide.
> Yet he, prime pattern of the captious art,
> Out-tibbalding poor *Tibbald*, tops his part;
> Holds high the scourge o'er each fam'd Author's head,
> Nor are their graves a refuge for the Dead.
> To *Milton* lending sense, to *Horace* wit,
> He makes 'em write what never poet writ:
> The *Roman Muse* arraigns his mangling pen,
> And *Paradise*, by him, is *lost* agen.
> Such was his doom impos'd by Heaven's decree,
> With ears that hear not, eyes that shall not see,
> The Low to raise, to level the Sublime,
> To blast all Beauty, and beprose all Rhyme.   (lines 127-42)

Pope apparently had these lines in mind when he wrote *Dunciad* IV, 211-14.

[13] For an account of Pope's edition of Shakespeare, see Chapter IV of Professor Austin Warren's *Alexander Pope as Critic and Humanist*, Princeton, 1929.

[14] There is a reference to this translation in the long note to I, 106.

[15] For a full account of Theobald one may read F. Jones, *Lewis Theobald, his Contribution to English Scholarship*, New York, 1919, and Chapters VII-X of T. R. Lounsbury's *The Text of Shakespeare*, New York, 1906.

[16] See the amusing note to I, 109.

[17] He had supplemented his *Shakespeare Restored* with further emendations contributed to the weekly journals.

[18] Note to II, 149.

NOTES TO CHAPTER VII

[1] Elwin-Courthope, VIII, 154-5. Fenton and Broome had been Pope's subordinate versifiers in the translation of the *Odyssey*.

[2] These same years, 1733-1735, produced a large harvest of ethical epistles, published like those of Pope in slender folios with large and handsome type. The following list includes merely those folio epistles which the present writer has had occasion to examine. It could doubtless be very considerably extended.

Of Modern Wit. An Epistle to the Right Honourable Sir William Young. London—Henry Lintot—1733.

An Essay on Faction. London—J. Peele—1733.

The Man of Taste. Occasion'd by an Epistle of Mr. Pope's on that Subject. By the Author of the Art of Politics [James Bramston]. London, 1733.

The Woman of Taste. Occasioned by a late Poem, entitled, The Man of Taste. By a Friend of the Author's—London—J. Batley, 1733.

Advice to a Lady. London: Lawton Gilliver, 1733. [By Lyttelton?]

The Modern Reasoners: An Epistle to a Friend. London—Lawton Gilliver—1734.

The Muse an Advocate for Injur'd Merit. In an Epistle to the Right Honourable Sir Robert Walpole. London—J. Roberts—1734.

Of Active and Retired Life, an Epistle. London—T. Cooper—1735.

An Essay on Reason [By Walter Harte], London, 1735.

Beauty: or the Art of Charming. A Poem. London—Lawton Gilliver—1735.

A View of the Town: in an Epistle to a Friend in the Country. A Satire—London—R. Penny, for the Author, and sold by A. Dodd—1735.

[3] In the address "To the Reader" prefixed to the first edition of Epistle I, the publisher says of the anonymous author:

> As he *imitates* no Man, so he would be thought to vye with no Man in these Epistles, particularly with the noted Author of TWO lately published.

[4] Johnson in his Life of Pope (*Lives of the English Poets*, ed. G. B. Hill, III, 161) gives this account of the matter:

> To those authors whom he had personally offended, and to those whose opinion the world considered as decisive, and whom he suspected of enmity or malevolence, he sent his *Essay* as a present before publication that they might defeat their own enmity by praises, which they could not afterwards decently retract.

For Pope's fears as to the charge of heterodoxy see his letters to Caryll dated March 8 and October 23, 1733, and January 1, 1734. (Elwin-Courthope, VI, 339, 345-7.)

[5] See Chapter VIII, note 5.

[6] Quoted by René Bray, *La Formation de la doctrine classique en France*, Paris, 1927, p. 69. This book is of primary importance for any student who wishes to understand the beginnings of neo-classical theory.

[7] *Works of Pope* (1797), III, 13.

[8] See Pope's letter to Caryll of October 23, 1733, Elwin-Courthope, VI, 346.

[9] For a detailed and very illuminating history of this idea, which from the Middle Ages to the end of the eighteenth century was one of the great controlling ideas of European thought, see A. O. Lovejoy's *The Great Chain of Being*, Cambridge, Mass., 1936.

[10] The *Essay on Man* was apparently widely read in the United States in the first half of the nineteenth century. The Huntington Library has the following early editions: Lansingburgh, N.Y., 1790 (MDCCLXL); Wor-

cester, Mass., 1797; Philadelphia, 1804; Pittsburgh, 1813; Exeter, N.H., 1818; Hallowell, Maine, 1819; Gardiner, Maine, 1824; Hartford, 1824, 1828; Portland, Maine, 1828, 1837, 1841; West Brookfield, Mass., 1843.

[11] Law's *A Serious Call to a Devout and Holy Life* first published in 1729, four years earlier than the *Essay on Man*, was responsible for turning the youthful Samuel Johnson to a life of deep devotion. See Boswell's *Life of Johnson*, ed. G. B. Hill, I, 68-9.

[12] Spence, p. 315.

[13] *Works of Lord Byron*, ed. R. E. Prothero, "Letters and Journals," V, 554.

NOTES TO CHAPTER VIII

[1] For a full and authoritative discussion of the matter see George Sherburn, "'Timons Villa' and Cannons," *Huntington Library Bulletin*, VIII, 131-52 (October, 1935). Professor Sherburn makes it highly improbable that Pope ever intended to ridicule Chandos, and also very improbable that Chandos had conferred any benefits on Pope beyond his subscription for twelve sets of the *Iliad*.

[2] *A Discourse concerning the Original and Progress of Satire* (1692), *Essays of John Dryden*, ed. Ker, II, 92-3.

[3] Professor Sherburn has shown that Pope had good reasons for so thinking. See *Early Career of Alexander Pope*, pp. 127-45.

[4] Did Pope, perhaps, remember these lines from the Duke of Buckingham's *Essay on Satire*:

> But with sharp Eyes those nicer Faults to find,
> Which lie obscurely in the wisest Mind,
> That little Speck, which all the rest will spoil; (33-5)

Works (edited by Pope) 1723, I, 113-26.

[5] In December, 1734, was published *Sober Advice from Horace to the Young Gentlemen about Town*. The title page states that it is an imitation "in the Manner of Mr. Pope"; but, though Pope never in so many words acknowledged it, there can be no doubt that it is his work. The dedication, "To Alexander Pope, Esq.," is all but an acknowledgment:

> Sir, I have so great a Trust in your Indulgence toward me, as to believe you cannot but Patronize this Imitation, so much in your own Manner, and whose Birth I may truly say is owing to you . . . . I hope you will believe that while I express my Regard for you, it is only out of Modesty I conceal my Name; since, tho' perhaps, I may not profess myself your Admirer, so much as some others, I cannot but be, with as much inward Respect, Good-will, and Zeal as any Man, *Dear Sir, Your most Affectionate* AND *Faithful Servant.*

The "sober advice" of Horace and of his imitator is that young gentlemen will find it safer and pleasanter to confine their amours to unmarried women. It would be beyond the mark to look for any serious satiric purpose in what is merely an exercise in playful ribaldry.

NOTES TO CHAPTER IX

[1] Volume I was the collected *Works* of 1717.

[2] As given in the edition of 1729.

[3] Argument to Book the Fourth.

[4] The "New Dunciad" of 1742 had broken off with a set of asterisks and the note, "De-est Finis." It would seem that Pope had already planned to transfer to the end of Book IV the concluding lines of Book III.

[5] His best known comedies are *Love's Last Shift* (1696) and *The Careless Husband* (1705).

[6] In 1741 Fielding mimicked the title in his "An Apology for the Life of Mrs. Shamela Andrews. . . . By Mr. Conny Keyber." The ridicule of Cibber, as well as that of Richardson, is continued in *Joseph Andrews* (1742).

[7] In 1740 was published "The Tryal of Colley Cibber, Comedian, &c. For writing a Book intitled An Apology for his Life, &c. Being A thorough examination thereof; wherein he is proved guilty of High Crimes and Misdemeanors against the English Language. . . ." The dedicatory letter is signed "T. Johnson."

[8] The full title is "A Blast upon Bays; Or, A New Lick at the Laureat. Containing, Remarks upon a Late Tattling Performance, entitled, A Letter from Mr. Cibber to Mr. Pope, &c." The small-paper quarto of 26 pages is dated at the end "July 29, 1742."

[9] This Advertisement in subsequent editions was relegated to an Appendix. It is given in Elwin-Courthope, IV, 237.

INDEX I

WRITINGS OF POPE

INDEX II
NAMES AND TOPICS

248 Index

Warton, Joseph, 58, 86, 92, ,118, 119
165
Welsted, Leonard, 154
Wesley, Charles, 182
Wesley, Samuel, 6
Weston, Mrs. (John), 90
Wharton, Duke of (Philip Wharton),
184

Wireker, Nigellus, 191
Wit *vs.* Judgment, 25-30, 86, 198-202
Wordsworth, William, 1, 11, 56, 61,
123, 163, 176, 180, 226
Wren, Sir Christopher, 107
Wycherley, William, 134

Young, Edward, 107, 135, 193, 200